# About Access Archaeology

*Access Archaeology* offers a different publishing model for specialist academic material that might traditionally prove commercially unviable, perhaps due to its sheer extent or volume of colour content, or simply due to its relatively niche field of interest. This could apply, for example, to a PhD dissertation or a catalogue of archaeological data.

All *Access Archaeology* publications are available in open-access e-pdf format and in print format. The open-access model supports dissemination in areas of the world where budgets are more severely limited, and also allows individual academics from all over the world the opportunity to access the material privately, rather than relying solely on their university or public library. Print copies, nevertheless, remain available to individuals and institutions who need or prefer them.

The material is refereed and/or peer reviewed. Copy-editing takes place prior to submission of the work for publication and is the responsibility of the author. Academics who are able to supply print-ready material are not charged any fee to publish (including making the material available in open-access). In some instances the material is type-set in-house and in these cases a small charge is passed on for layout work.

Our principal effort goes into promoting the material, both in open-access and print, where *Access Archaeology* books get the same level of attention as all of our publications which are marketed through e-alerts, print catalogues, displays at academic conferences, and are supported by professional distribution worldwide.

Open-access allows for greater dissemination of academic work than traditional print models could ever hope to support. It is common for an open-access e-pdf to be downloaded hundreds or sometimes thousands of times when it first appears on our website. Print sales of such specialist material would take years to match this figure, if indeed they ever would.

This model may well evolve over time, but its ambition will always remain to publish archaeological material that would prove commercially unviable in traditional publishing models, without passing the expense on to the academic (author or reader).

# Identifying Brúnanburh:
## *ón dyngesmere* –
## the sea of noise

John R. Kirby

Access Archaeology

ARCHAEOPRESS PUBLISHING LTD
Summertown Pavilion
18-24 Middle Way
Summertown
Oxford OX2 7LG

www.archaeopress.com

ISBN 978-1-78969-107-8
ISBN 978-1-78969-108-5 (e-Pdf)

© Archaeopress and J R Kirby 2019

Cover: Abingdon Sword Hilt © J.R.Kirby 2007

Printed and bound in Great Britain by
Marston Book Services Ltd, Oxfordshire

All rights reserved. No part of this book may be reproduced, stored in retrieval system, or transmitted, in any form or by any means, electronic, mechanical, photocopying or otherwise, without the prior written permission of the copyright owners.

This book is available direct from Archaeopress or from our website www.archaeopress.com

# Acknowledgements

The author wishes to kindly acknowledge the most gracious and benevolent travel funding for this article which was assisted by a grant from the Ancient World Research Cluster at Wolfson College, Oxford, who are generously supported by a gift from the Lorne Thyssen Research Fund.

Dedicated to my father and mother

After the battle a Christian warrior skáld could have replied thus to his friend King Æthelstan

*"Sól gengr i aegi*
*hjarta mitt var runnit sundr í siga*
*segja leið, gjálfr-stoð*
*Segjanda er allt vin sinum*
*sóma-mađr*

*"The sun sinks into the sea*
*My heart was molten into drops*
*Lead the way, steeds of the sea*
*All can be said of a friend*
*An honourable, respectable man"*

# CONTENTS

| | |
|---|---|
| INTRODUCTION | 5 |
| EXPLANATION OF CLIMATIC PHRASES IN THE POEM | 6 |
|     FIRST POINT | 6 |
| MARITIME AND METEOROLOGICAL CONDITIONS | 7 |
|     SECOND POINT | 8 |
|     THIRD POINT | 11 |
|     FOURTH POINT | 14 |
| COMPARISON OF HISTORICAL ANNALS WITH METEOROLOGICAL CONDITIONS.. | 17 |
|     FIFTH POINT | 17 |
| NEW EVIDENCE – THE FYLDE ARGUMENT | 18 |
|     LANDSCAPE ANALYSIS | 18 |
|     FIELD-NAMES ON AMOUNDERNESS – THE BATTLE ON THE PLAIN | 22 |
|     FIELD-NAMES AROUND TREALES AND LUNDR – THE FIRST BATTLE | 24 |
|     FIELD-NAMES OF BERGERODE / *BRÚNE* - THE SECOND & FINAL BATTLE | 27 |
| SOCIO-POLITICS IN THE NORTH-WEST | 31 |
| A DISCRETE ANALYSIS – DNA ANALYSIS | 34 |
| THE FALSE ANALYSIS – THE BROMBOROUGH ARGUMENT | 36 |
| BIBLIOGRAPHY | 39 |

# List of Figures

Figure. 1. LANDSAT Image highlighting Morecambe Bay, Bay of Lune and the top part of Amounderness............8

Figure. 2. Aerial photograph showing the present day 'surge' at the Walney Meetings before it goes under the Vickers Bridge....................9

Figure 3. Tidal surges – the isle of Barrow in 1851, pre-industrial revolution ............10

Figure 4. Predicted Chart Datum of the tidal disposition for the year AD 937............11

Figure 5. Predicted Tidal Disposition for September AD937 ............12

Figure 6. The Bathymetry of Morecambe Bay ............14

Figure 7. The Lune Deep, Morecambe Bay ............14

Figure 8. Action of vortices created from singularities on the seabed ............16

Figure 9. Irish Sea with Lancashire coastline highlighting Cyclonic Low Pressure in Morecambe Bay and Amounderness............17

Figure 10. Climate data for Blackpool............18

Figure 11. 1577 Saxton, Christopher. *Lancastriae comitatus palatinus*............19

Figure 12. 1753 (Map 4A) Morden, Robert. 'The County Palatine of Lancaster' (1695) final state of Morden's large map from Camden's *Britannia* (London, 1753)............19

Figure 13. Base map the *'Fylde and Wyre Antiquarian Society'* assessment ............21

Figure 14. A distance of one mile separates Treales and Lund ............21

Figure 15. Field System between Kirkham, Treales and Lund ............23

Figure 16. Detail. Treales and Dowbridge Area............23

Figure 17. Detail. Deepdale Wood and the Moor a continuation of Fulwood Moor north of Preston ............23

Figure 18. Tithe Map of Thornton by Thomas Hull 1839 ............29

Figure 19. Detail of Tithe Map............29

Figure 20. Butts Lane surrounding the Borty Berry Fields of the burgh............29

Figure 21. Field-names between *Trunnah Fields* and *Borty Berry Fields* ............30

Figure 22. Line of Anglo-Saxon forts blocking the Scottish and Northern Welsh armies from fleeing north............32

Figure 23. Note *Bergerod*. Image taken from "Great Britain's Coastal Pilot" produced by Captain Greenville Collins RN. Fylde Coast 1689 ............32

# Abbreviations

| | |
|---|---|
| AClon | Annals of Clonmacnoise |
| AngloDan | Anglo-Danish |
| adj. | adjective |
| AFM | Annals of the Kingdom of Ireland by the Four Masters |
| AIn | Annals of Innisfalen |
| ARF | Annals Regni Francorum |
| ASax | Anglo-Saxon |
| ASC | Anglo-Saxon Chronicles |
| AU | Annals of Ulster |
| B&T | Bosworth & Toller |
| Com Scand | Common Scandinavian |
| CVC | Cleasby, Vigfusson and Craigie |
| DAMTP | Dept., of Applied Mathematics & Theoretical Physics (Cambridge) |
| DB | Domesday Book |
| EE | Eilert Ekwall |
| ESA | European Space Agency |
| Gk | Greek |
| HH | Henry of Huntingdon |
| HM | Her Majesty |
| L&S | Liddle & Scott |
| Mod Eng | Modern English |
| MS | Manuscript |
| n | noun |
| ODan | Old Danish |
| OE | Old English |
| ME | Middle English |
| OIc | Old Icelandic |
| OIrish | Old Irish |
| ON | Old Norse |
| OScot | Old Scottish |
| NASA | National Aeronautics and Space Administration |
| PIE | Proto Indo-European |
| PN | Place Name |
| RN | Royal Navy |
| R&S | Rivet & Smith |
| RW | Roger of Wendover |
| VLF | Very Low Frequency |
| WW | F.T.Wainwright |

# Identifying Brúnanburh:
## *ón dyngesmere* – the sea of noise.
John R. Kirby

### INTRODUCTION

Few events of the Early Medieval Age have created such controversy amongst scholars as the Battle of *Brúnanburh* for the kingdom of England (AD 937). The location of this battle, undiscovered in the mists of time, almost epitomizes the spurious term 'Dark Ages'[1].

Evidence is at the heart of this problem. The methodology of this article gathers evidence for the identification of this battle from scientific, literary, archaeological, historical and genealogical disciplines. This analysis of the MSS offers a new approach for detecting the *Brúnanburh* site through verifiable appraisal from these domains. Verification of climatic maritime phrases in the MSS eventually identifying the coastal landscape is possible, for crucially it should be stated that **'manuscript evidence is material culture'**. Phrases within the poem highlight a loud noise from the sea which has been regarded by some scholars as a 'red herring' - this must be investigated. Could this noise hold the key to the locale? Described as *'ón dyngesmere'* in the poem, this noise can be found in one unique locale – Morecambe Bay. Comparison of scientific with historical analysis offers a paradigm which can **verify** the actual site.

Various sites have been proposed for *Æthelstan's* battle against the Hiberno-Norse alliance. The author noticed that for over two centuries scholars have chosen different positions (the latest are: P. Cavill[2], S. Harding & M. Jobling[3], C. Hart[4], A. P. Smyth[5], M. Wood[6], A. Breeze[7] etc). There is no point in reiterating their arguments that state their selected place-name for *Brúnanburh;* these became their starting point for their individual theories but this author will advance a valid case from maritime and landscape phrases in the poem. For there are a plethora of similar place-names for *Brúnanburh* in the north of England. Consequently, this has only created confusion. Bromborough is the latest theory but again this is very doubtful as there are many inaccuracies.

---

[1.] A term first coined by Petrarch circa 1350. Theodore E. Mommsen, "Petrarch's Conception of the 'Dark Ages'" *Speculum* **17**.2 (April 1942: 226–242). See also, Eisner, M. 2014 Renaissance Quarterly 67 755-90.

[2.] For the Bromborough (Cheshire) argument see: Cavill, Paul, Harding, Stephen & Jesch, Judith 2004 *Revisiting Dingesmere.* Journal of the English Place-Name Society xxxvi pp25-38. See also Cavill, Paul 2008 *The site of the Battle of Brunanburh: manuscripts and maps, grammar and geography.* In A Commodity of Good Names: Essays in honour of Margaret Gelling (eds.) Padel, O.J. & Parsons, D.N., Shaun Tyas,

[3.] Also for the Bromborough argument see: Harding, S., Jobling, M. 2008 *Vikings.* British Archaeology. (Nov-Dec). Wood, M. 2013 p143 makes the point "It is unlikely to have been in the heartland of Mercia."

[4.] For the Bourn (Lincolnshire) argument: Hart, Cyril. 1992 *The Danelaw.* The Hambledon Press, London.

[5.] For the Bruneswald (Northamptonshire) argument: Smyth, Alfred P. 1979 *Scandinavian York & Dublin, the History and Archaeology of Two Related Viking Kingdoms.* Vol. 2, Humanities Press: New Jersey & Templekieran Press: Dublin.

[6.] For the Brinsworth (South Yorkshire) argument: Wood, Michael 1980 *Brunanburh Revisited.* Saga Book of the Viking Society xx.3 pp200-17. See, Wood, M. 2013 Yorks. Arch. Journ. 85 pp138-59, this Humber argument of *Anlaf (Óláfr)* travelling over the Pentland Firth or the Firth of Forth from climatic and maritime aspects become untenable. Wood maintains that the River Went was a derivation of Wendun where the battle was fought, but again there is no valid evidence and the confusion of place-names continues.

[7.] Breeze, Andrew. 1999 *The Battle of Brunanburh and Welsh Tradition.* Neophilologus 83: 479-482. Notice the interesting development of the Welsh *kattybrudawt* / O Brythonic *cattybrunawc.* However, Breeze has a different outcome though for the locale of *Brúnanburh.*

# EXPLANATION OF CLIMATIC PHRASES IN THE POEM

Challenging these inaccuracies proved thought-provoking. The *Brúnanburh* poem revealed three phrases that appear to represent a locale and point to climatic conditions – qualification of the physical type, the result created, and the transient sound, for one naturally leads to the other. The phrase 'ón dyngesmere' (line 55) in the Anglo-Saxon poem was analysed by Thorpe in 1834[8], Garnett in 1889[9] and Cockburn in 1931[10] who proposed that *dynges* was *dines* (MS Cotton Otho B. xi.)[11] meaning 'noise' giving rise to 'the noisy sea', or 'sea of noise' and they all agree on this interpretation. [ASax. **dynge, dynige, es**, m? *A noise, dashing, storm; sonus, strepitus, procella, Ón dynges mere, on the sea of noise*][12] (see note 12 below: **ding**, e; f. *A dungeon, prison.* Possibly the two forms represent a literary device - a kenning,). Magoun in 1933[13] reviewed Cockburn, he followed Guest's argument of 1838[14] and called *dyngesmere* 'the resounding sea', but Guest chose the Browney, Durham area which cannot be correct. In 1938 Campbell[15] equated these phrases, **ón dyngesmere** and **ón fealene flod**, with an estuary of dark water and sand. However, none were able to identify the locale, although most describe *dyngesmere* as variations of a sea of noise. Could tangible evidence confirm the historical MS? The following five points highlight topographical references in the poem.

**The first point:** that climatic maritime appraisal has been largely ignored in the hunt for the locale of *Brúnanburh*. A loud rumbling noise from the sea around Morecambe Bay has been regarded by some scholars as a 'red herring', yet such a noise exists. As this 'sea of noise' was a distinct localized feature it may also be the 'estuary of dark water' highlighted by Campbell. There are three phrases in the poem that describe climatic features and correlation with *Brúnanburh* becomes significant. These three couplets represent a specific event, whereas many scholars have taken the last couplet only. See lines 27-28, 36-37, and 55-56 below,

| | | |
|---|---|---|
| "þae mid anlafe **ofer æra gebland** ón lides bosme land gesohtun" | who came with Anlaf over the **sea-surge** in the bosom of a ship, those who sought land, | **Thorpe:** O'er the waves mingling |
| "cread cnearen flot cyning ut gewat **ón fealene flod** feorh generede" | he pressed the ship afloat, the king went out on the **dusky flood-tide,** he saved his life. | **Thorpe:** on the fallow flood |
| "dreorig daroða laf **ón dyngesmere** ofer deop wæter difel in secan" | dejected survivors of battle, **on the sea of noise** over waters deep sought Dublin, | **Thorpe:** on the roaring sea |

[8.] Thorpe's translation is remarkably close to a modern Fluid Dynamic sense especially lines 27-8: Thorpe, Benjamin 1861 *Anglo-Saxon Chronicles* Ed Benjamin Thorpe Vol II, London, pp86-88. But see *Florence of Worcester* (ed.) Thorpe, B. 1848. Óláfr enters York at a later time. (see *Historia Regum* in *Historia Dunelmensis Ecclesiae Symeonis Opera.*, ii, 93).

[9.] Garnett, James M. 1889, ed. 1901 *Elene; Judith; Athelstan, or the fight at Brunanburh; Byrhtnoth, or the fight at Maldon; and the Dream of the Rood: Anglo-Saxon Poems.* Boston, Ginn & Co. Athenaeum Press, 57-59.

[10.] Cockburn, John H.1931 *The battle of Brunanburgh and its period elucidated by place-names.* London & Sheffield. Cockburn pursued Armitage Goodall's (1914, 312-313) Brinsworth argument (see M. Wood 2013).

[11.] British Library MS Cotton Otho B. xi, London.

[12.] Bosworth & Toller revised Toller 1898, *Anglo Saxon Dictionary*. O.U.P. (Main Volume p221). See also p.205 **ding**, e; f. *A dungeon, prison; carcer* :-- *Com hæleða þreat to ðære dimman ding* - the troop of heroes came to the dark dungeon, Andr. Kmbl. 2541. This suggests trapping the remnants of the army in the mere, possibly a play of the words which the Anglo-Saxons loved.

[13.] Magoun, F. P. 1933 *Cockburn: the battle of Brunanburh and its period elucidated by place-names.* 86 n.1.

[14.] Guest, Edwin. 1838 *History of English Rhythms.* Vol II London, Will. Pickering. Guest chose Browney.

[15.] Campbell, Alistair 1938 *The Battle of Brunanburh*, London.

Halloran's argument in 2005[16] for *dyngesmere* cannot be sustained. These three couplets emphasize the device of alliteration, employed to create a rhythmical sound especially in the last couplet and place stress on the word *dyngesmere*, - clearly it is 'd' not 'þ' mentioned by Cavill et al, in 2004 p.29[17]; 2008[18]. Placing 'þ' instead of 'd' for *dynges* 'storm', would change the intention of the word to *þing* 'assembly, a meeting, a court'. Such a change would destroy not only the alliteration but the sense of the couplet. As *dynges* is employed in a maritime context it must be regarded as a specific word relevant to an estuary. This seems to have been forgotten for more 'land based' words, personal-names, and the use of 'þ' which lacks conviction. The 'þ' / 'T' (cf *Thingwall*) represents a later Anglo-Norman pronunciation occurring later than AD 937. Note the first letter 'd' in 'difel' the MSS is lower case and alliterates with 'dyngesmere', also the three couplets show end rhyme. Yet, although both Dodgson and Cavill suggest '*dyngesmere*' might be derived from the river-name Dee, Dodgson's remark in 1972 (PNCh, 4. 240) [19] and his addition in Addenda and Corrigenda 1997 (PNCh, 5:2 xxi) [20], citing the similarity of **gē** 'district' and ***ingas*** 'the people of'; *Gē-ing-*formation has contracted to *Gēng-* and *Gīng-*; while this appears to be true to this name, it is a big jump to say that *dinges, dynges,* reacts in the same way especially as a surrogate name *dyngesmere*. *Ge-ingas mere*, 'the district of the people of the mere'. This would mean the marshy area below Heswall was the locale but it does not constitute a Plain. (The poem states: *gefylde* plus *waelfelda* – 'the plain of the slain' - see page 15). Yet, if Dodgson's argument was correct then the name of the battle would be *Heswall* not *Brúnanburh*. We are actually left with 'the sound from the *mere*/noisy storm'; the idea of which scholars seem reluctant to entertain not understanding the fluid dynamics of severe sea surge conditions. Because Cavill (2004 p26) cannot understand the physical aspects of fluid dynamics he dismisses it with this sentence, *"the Sea of Noise does not make overmuch sense as a name at all."*

The science of fluid dynamics demonstrates the specific use of *dynges* meaning 'sound from the *mere*/noisy storm' which indicates an area of severe maritime danger for those that use this coastal area. The battle was fought in Northumbria, (Camden 1607 emphasized a Northumbrian connection), therefore above the Mercia / Northumbria border i.e. the river Ribble. From this analysis, Morecambe Bay appears to be the '*mere*' that is described in the poem. Can a maritime analysis of Morecambe Bay (Figure 1 p8) confirm this theory?

---

[16]. Halloran, Kevin, 2005 *The Brunanburh Campaign: A Reappraisal,* Scottish Historical Review Vol. LXXXIV, 2: No.218 (October), 146. Halloran's Brúnanburh/Burnswark argument was already disproved by General W. Roy. See Christison, D. 1899 Proceedings of the Society of Antiquaries of Scotland, 198-218, (1898).

[17]. Cavill et al, 2004 Journal of the English Place-Names Society *"Revisiting dingesmere"* xxxvi 25-38. The graphic description of the poem can enthusiastically misdirect one, overlooking the simple phrases.

[18]. Cavill Paul 2008 *The site of the Battle of Brunanburh: manuscripts and maps, grammar and geography.* In A Commodity of Good Names: Essays in honour of Margaret Gelling (eds.) Padel, O.J. & Parsons, D.N.

[19]. Dodgson, John McN. 1972 *Place-Names of Cheshire,* 4. 240. Wood, M. 2013 states, "For the historian of the tenth century, however, to place Brunanburh on the shore of the Mersey raises many intractable problems with the sources, none of which (as Dodgson himself saw) supports a location in the Wirral."

[20]. Dodgson, John McN. 1997 *Addenda and Corrigenda Place-Names of Cheshire,* 5:2 xxi.

**Figure. 1.** LANDSAT Image highlighting Morecambe Bay, Bay of Lune and the top part of Amounderness. (*Copyright National Remote Sensing Centre Ltd. Raw data. Copyright. European Space Agency / Eurimage*).[21]

## MARITIME AND METEOROLOGICAL CONDITIONS

**The second point:** that topographically *dyngesmere* implies an estuary, a shallow sea; the next phrase *ofer deóp wæter* qualifies a change of environment to that of an ocean. It cannot be the version proposed by Cavill et al (2004 p36: *Thingsbyvollr/Þings-mere* described by them as 'wetland by the Thing'[22]). Noticeably, there is no use of the suffix '-by' in Thingwall. The distinctively alliterative style, can create words which are abstruse surrogate kennings. A literal interpretation of 'storm' would indicate 'tempest or surge'. Alternatively, *dynges* may have a double meaning, *ding* – dungeon and imply therefore 'clashing and trapped', the sound is like the battle over the *mere* – a kenning, a type of trope. Research by this author did confirm that 'loud noises' emanated from Morecambe Bay during equinox surges and extremely adverse weather conditions. What is the evidence within the area of Morecambe Bay?

21. LANDSAT Image. *Copyright National Remote Sensing Centre Ltd. Raw data. Copyright. European Space Agency/Eurimage.*

22. Cavill et al, 2004 Journal of the English Place-Names Society *"Revisiting dingesmere"* 36: 25-38 p.36.

Germane to this question Ekwall, in 1922[23] described the Isle of Barrow in the north-west of Morecambe Bay as a surrogate, Celtic *Barr* and ON -*ey* Barley Isle. Yet, there are good reasons for suggesting this meaning may be incorrect: that it derived from Com Scand. *bára* 'wave, swell, surge, billow island' (Figure 2). As all the other isles (see Ekwall 1922) are distinctly Com. Scandinavian (c. AD 700 – 860) it would follow logically that Barrey would have a Com. Scandinavian origin *bára* < *Børrey*[24] which has been dialectically changed *bára* < *Børrey* to *Barrey* (see Figure 2, and Figure 3, p.10 below). Comparison with the ancient Greek seafaring word Κύμα a wave, billow, swell, (Liddle & Scott 1883:858ab[25]) is similar to that of the O.Ic. *bára* a wave, billow, swell. (C.V.C.1952:54b[26]). Morton (2001:31[27]) highlights wave 'refraction' "The heightening and steepening of waves as they approach the shore is commonly referred to in ancient literature as early as the Iliad":

> "..... like a crag sheer and great, hard by the grey sea, that abides the swift paths of the shrill winds and the swollen waves (κύματα τι τροφοεντα) that belch forth against it; even the Danaans withstood the Trojan steadfastly. (Hom Il. 15.619-622; compare Il 4.422-6)."

**Figure. 2.** Aerial photograph showing the present day 'surge' at the Walney Meetings before it goes under the Vickers Bridge seen at the bottom of this picture. (*Imagery©2015 Infoterra LTD & Bluesky, Landsat, Data SIO, NOAA, U.S. Navy GEBCO. Map Data © 2015 Google*).

---

[23]. Ekwall, Eilert 1922 *Place Names of Lancashire.* Manchester University Press, p204. Surges occur in normal high tides up the rivers Kent and Leven in the form of bores.

[24]. Haugen, Einar 1976 *The Scandinavian Languages: an introduction to their history.* Faber & Faber. London. 6.3. (10). p.73.

[25]. Liddle, Henry G. & Scott, Robert 1883 *Greek-English Lexicon.* New York: 858ab. The similarity of these two words (O.Ic. *bára* and Gk. Κύμα) may take us back to the Migration Age or even further to 950 BC – 1200 BC.

[26]. Cleasby, R., Vígfússon, G. & Craigie, R. 1957 *Icelandic English Dictionary.* O.U.P.

[27]. Morton, Jamie 2001 *The Role of the Physical Environment in Ancient Greek Seafaring.* Brill, Leiden, :31.

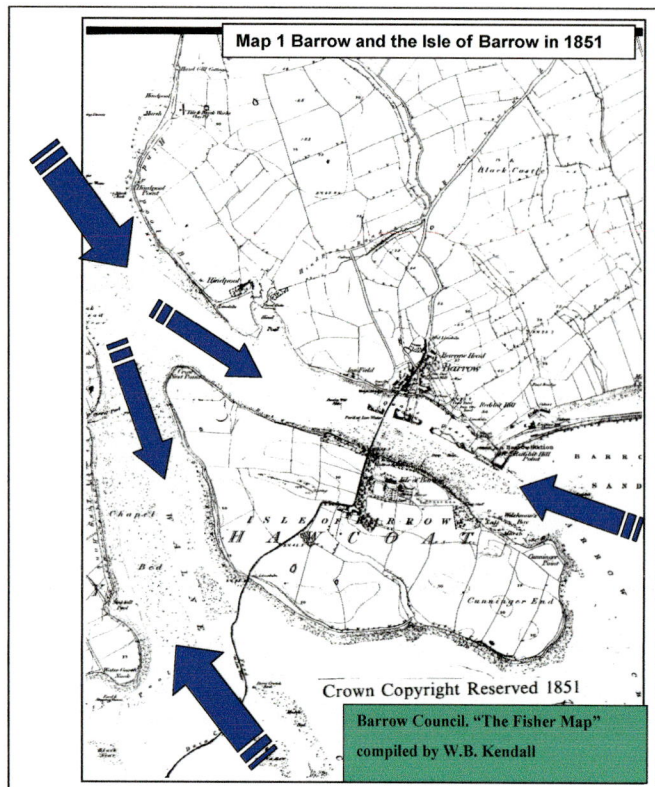

**Map 1** Barrow and the Isle of Barrow in 1851
Crown Copyright Reserved 1851
Barrow Council. "The Fisher Map" compiled by W.B. Kendall

**Figure 3.** TIDAL SURGES – the isle of Barrow in 1851, pre-industrial revolution.

Morecambe Bay (derived from Ptolemy's Itinerary *Morikámbē*, suggested by John Whitaker in 1771)[28] covers an area of 310km² of intertidal sandflats and mudflats. Large tidal range occurs up to 10.5 metres to Chart Datum. At spring tides and during the equinox this Chart Datum is exceeded by 2.5 – 3 metres. Tidal surges in this area can reach speeds of up to 9 knots. Where the surge separates around the Isle and both meet each other a collision speed of 18 knots can occur. In extreme weather conditions the turbulence created by the friction of deep seabed depressions of Morecambe Bay allow 'trains' of waves to break at different times creating a loud noise. Also the tidal bores from the surge through the Barrow Channel create a noticeably loud noise. This was more pronounced before the Industrial fill in of the northern channel around the Isle of Barrow.

*N.B. Map out of copyright but with grateful thanks to Barrow Council.*

Wave 'refraction' is but one aspect of the physical events that occur[29], when other aspects like the severe weather conditions of high winds, coupled with a cyclonic low transpire at the equinox high tide over the unusual seabed of Morecambe Bay strange sounds occur. This aspect combined with strong currents of heavy saline inflowing seawater pushing over the shallow mud-banks form a speedy 'race' but slow-down in deeper water depressions. These features are further accentuated by the outflowing lighter fresh water from five rivers which create violent turbulence. After hearing the actual noise from the Bay plus seeing the surge going under the Vickers Bridge, this aspect of Maritime archaeology was explored by the author who liaised with the Admiralty, (see figures 4 and 5)[30], assessing the estimated Chart Datum values with regards the tidal dispositions of Morecambe Bay in the year AD 937. The project was enabled by using the NASA database and the resultant data confirmed the author's argument. The equinox tides when combined with a cyclonic Low Pressure create peak surge conditions of 2.5 -3.5 metres above the Chart Datum, (i.e. above the normal high tide), conditions necessary for this peculiar noise to be heard. M. Deacon[31] explored the history of surges from Pliny the Elder to Newton in some detail. Newton established laws and highlights semidiurnal tides, the ranges of which occur when the spring tides (*syzygy*) correspond with the lunar perigee described by F. J. Wood[32].

[28.] Whitaker, John 1771 *History of Manchester in four books,* Vol. 1, 125.

[29.] The 'heightening and steepening of the waves' as they approach the various mudbank depressions of Morecambe Bay estuary alters the wave shape creating noise when high winds occur.

[30] RN Nautical Almanac Office, Taunton. Licence Ref. No.557909. Thanks to Christopher Jones, (Head of Tides, UK Hydrographic Office), Steve Cooper and George Huish 2012. This article pages 11 and 12.

[31.] Deacon, Margaret 1971 *Scientists and the Sea 1650-1900.* London: Academic Press.

[32.] Wood, F. J. 1986 *Tidal Dynamics, Coastal Flooding and Cycles of Gravitational Force.* Dordrecht: D. Reidel.

**The third point:** scientific analysis of the tidal surge was undertaken by projecting a model of past equinox tides during the early part of the 10th century (see Figure 4) by the Admiralty at HM Nautical Almanac Office. Their conclusions verified these above statements. The surge occurs today over the Walney Meetings (see Figure 3, p.10) plus the stony Chapel Beds, but loud ambient noises are heard from the turbulence in Morecambe Bay as the surge funnels up the Leven and Kent Estuaries creating tidal bores. It should be noted that the tidal range exceeds 10m in height, reaching at times 14m in severe storm conditions. Christopher Jones, (Head of Tides, UK Hydrographic Office, 2012), stated that notice should be taken of the following:

"These are predicted values only – not observed tidal data. Thus, *no realistic account can be taken of any meteorological effects, which may have been prevalent on those days. These wind and pressure effects can significantly alter the observed tide, causing it to deviate considerably from the predicted values.* Additionally, the predictions are based on data derived from relatively recent tidal observations at Heysham; *owing to the age of the requested time period, physical and geographic conditions in the estuary may well have been quite different to those today.* Such physical conditions include the shape, size and depth of the estuary which in turn would affect the resonance of the tidal signal propagating within it, and ultimately the tide times and ranges accordingly." Recent analysis demonstrates this aspect, George Huish of the UK Hydrographic Office states, "In January 1991 a surge peak of 2.3m was recorded at Heysham (i.e. above Chart Datum)".

***Heysham, Morecambe Bay*** (©: *British Crown Jan 2012*, Admiralty, RN Nautical Almanac Office, Taunton. Lic. Ref. No. 557909)
## "Extreme Tides" for the year AD 937

Annual extremes for 0937 (m)

| 20/04/937 18:59 | 0.4 | 28/10/937 23:46 | 10.6 |

Normal Chart Datum for High Tides

Monthly extremes for 0937 (m)

| January | 06/01/937 19:03 | 1.1 | 06/01/937 12:10 | 9.9 |
|---|---|---|---|---|
| February | 21/02/937 19:41 | 0.7 | 21/02/937 12:53 | 10.3 |
| March | 22/03/937 19:21 | 0.4 | 22/03/937 12:32 | 10.5 |
| April | 20/04/937 18:59 | 0.4 | 20/04/937 12:11 | 10.5 |
| May | 20/05/937 07:07 | 0.6 | 19/05/937 11:53 | 10.3 |
| June | 18/06/937 06:55 | 0.7 | 18/06/937 00:00 | 10.0 |
| July | 17/07/937 06:43 | 0.8 | 16/07/937 23:48 | 9.9 |
| August | 15/08/937 06:28 | 0.9 | 30/08/937 23:51 | 10.0 |
| September | 30/09/937 06:54 | 0.7 | 30/09/937 00:07 | 10.5 |
| October | 29/10/937 06:31 | 0.7 | 28/10/937 23:46 | 10.6 |
| November | 27/11/937 18:41 | 0.8 | 26/11/937 23:28 | 10.4 |
| December | 27/12/937 19:22 | 0.8 | 27/12/937 12:25 | 10.2 |

**Figure 4.** Predicted Chart Datum of the tidal disposition for the year AD 937. The thick square and represent the time of year when the battle took place. Although the equinox occurs in March and September the latter month is correct. (*Grateful thanks to the Admiralty, RN Nautical Almanac Office, Chris Jones, Steve Cooper and George Huish*).

What is known from historical record is recorded in the Annals of the Four Masters. A.P. Smyth[33] mentions OIrish: *Amhlaoibh /Anlaf* (Com Scand: *Óláfr*) in Northumbria between September and October. The Annals of the Four Masters[34] [AFM 935.16 corrected to AD 937] state, *Amhlaoibh, mac Gofradha, tighearna Gall, dothiachtain im Lughnasadh ó Ath Cliath, co rucc Amhlaoibh Cendcairech do Loch Ribh Leis & na Gaill báttar lais, .i. la Cairech, iar m-briseadh a long;* See also the Annals of Ulster[35] [AU] dated to AD 937 mention *Anlaf* raiding in Ireland during the summer of AD 937 around Lough Ree. Therefore, *Anlaf* could not have been in Northumbria earlier than Sept 937.

```
Heysham
54°02'N 2°55'W England    September 937
Times in GMT; heights in Metres above CD

01/09/937                10/09/937                19/09/937                28/09/937 Full Moon
High  00:30  10.2 m      High  09:32  8.8 m      High  02:38  8.3 m      High  11:10  9.9 m
High  12:52   9.8 m      High  21:53  9.2 m      High  15:01  8.1 m      High  23:27 10.3 m
Low   07:17   0.9 m      Low   03:53  1.7 m      Low   09:13  2.6 m      Low   05:31  1.0 m
Low   19:31   1.1 m      Low   16:12  1.9 m      Low   21:29  2.8 m      Low   17:48  1.1 m

02/09/937                11/09/937                20/09/937 First         29/09/937
High  01:10  10.1 m      High  10:19  9.2 m      Quarter                  High  11:49 10.1 m
High  13:32   9.7 m      High  22:36  9.6 m      High  03:19  7.8 m      Low   06:12  0.7 m
Low   07:56   0.9 m      Low   04:46  1.4 m      High  15:48  7.6 m      Low   18:29  0.9 m
Low   20:12   1.2 m      Low   16:59  1.6 m      Low   09:56  3.1 m
                                                  Low   22:22  3.3 m      30/09/937
03/09/937                12/09/937 New                                     High  00:07 10.5 m
High  01:52   9.9 m      Moon                     21/09/937                High  12:29 10.2 m
High  14:15   9.4 m      High  11:00  9.5 m      High  04:13  7.2 m      Low   06:54  0.7 m
Low   08:36   1.2 m      High  23:16  9.8 m      High  16:54  7.2 m      Low   19:12  0.9 m
Low   20:55   1.5 m      Low   05:30  1.1 m      Low   10:57  3.5 m
                         Low   17:38  1.4 m      Low   23:38  3.5 m
04/09/937
High  02:38   9.5 m      13/09/937                22/09/937
High  15:02   8.9 m      High  11:37  9.6 m      High  05:34  6.9 m
Low   09:19   1.5 m      High  23:52  9.8 m      High  18:23  7.1 m
Low   21:43   1.9 m      Low   06:08  1.1 m      Low   12:25  3.6 m
                         Low   18:12  1.4 m
05/09/937 Last                                    23/09/937
Quarter                  14/09/937                High  07:10  7.0 m
High  03:29   8.9 m      High  12:12  9.6 m      High  19:44  7.5 m
High  15:58   8.4 m      Low   06:41  1.1 m      Low   01:07  3.4 m
Low   10:09   2.0 m      Low   18:44  1.4 m      Low   13:46  3.4 m
Low   22:42   2.3 m
                         15/09/937                24/09/937
06/09/937                High  00:26  9.7 m      High  08:22  7.6 m
High  04:32   8.3 m      High  12:45  9.5 m      High  20:42  8.2 m
High  17:09   8.0 m      Low   07:13  1.3 m      Low   02:20  2.9 m
Low   11:13   2.5 m      Low   19:14  1.5 m      Low   14:49  2.8 m
Low   23:59   2.6 m
                         16/09/937                25/09/937
07/09/937                High  00:59  9.5 m      High  09:12  8.3 m
High  05:52   7.9 m      High  13:17  9.3 m      High  21:27  8.9 m
High  18:36   7.8 m      Low   07:42  1.5 m      Low   03:17  2.3 m
Low   12:37   2.8 m      Low   19:44  1.7 m      Low   15:41  2.3 m

08/09/937                17/09/937                26/09/937
High  07:20   7.9 m      High  01:31  9.2 m      High  09:53  8.9 m
High  19:58   8.2 m      High  13:50  8.9 m      High  22:08  9.5 m
Low   01:27   2.6 m      Low   08:10  1.8 m      Low   04:06  1.8 m
Low   14:02   2.6 m      Low   20:15  2.1 m      Low   16:25  1.8 m

09/09/937                18/09/937                27/09/937
High  08:34   8.3 m      High  02:04  8.8 m      High  10:32  9.5 m
High  21:02   8.7 m      High  14:23  8.6 m      High  22:47 10.0 m
Low   02:47   2.2 m      Low   08:39  2.2 m      Low   04:50  1.3 m
Low   15:14   2.3 m      Low   20:48  2.4 m      Low   17:07  1.4 m

                    British Crown Copyright © 2011
```

**Figure 5.** Predicted Tidal Disposition for September AD937 modelled by RN Nautical Almanac Office, Dec. 2011, using the NASA database. (Copyright: British Crown Jan. 2012, Admiralty, RN Nautical Almanac Office, Taunton. Lic. Ref. No.557909 Grateful thanks to Chris Jones, Steve Cooper and George Huish)[36]

"Although the model was based on predicted Chart Datum values note should be taken that in the 10$^{th}$ century surges, resonance and weather patterns were more severe than the present day. While these values are for normal Chart Datum, at the equinox a surge peak coupled with a cyclonic low pressure, increases the height by as much as 2.5 – 3.5 metres above the Chart Datum". (Pugh 1987 rept. 1996[37]; see also Environment Agency' Evidence Directorate and Defra Flood and Coastal Erosion Risk Management Research and Development Programme 2011 Project: SCV060064/TR2 Design sea levels[38]).

---

[33.] Smyth, Alfred P. 1979 *Scandinavian York & Dublin, the History and Archaeology of Two Related Viking Kingdoms.* Vol. 2, Humanities Press: New Jersey & Templekieran Press: Dublin.

[34.] Annals of the Kingdom of Ireland by the Four Masters, 7 vols (Dublin 1848-55) [AFM] J.P. O'Donovan (Ed & Trans), i 632 (AD 935.16).

[35.] Annals of Ulster (to AD 1131) part I Dublin 1983 [AU] AD 937.6, Sean Mac Airt & Gearoid Mac Niocaill (eds).

[36.] Copyright: British Crown Jan. 2012, Admiralty, RN Nautical Almanac Office, Taunton. Lic. Ref. No.557909. Grateful thanks to Chris Jones, Steve Cooper and George Huish.

[37.] Pugh. David 1987 (rept. 1996) *Tides, Surges and Mean Sea-level.* Natural Environment Research Council, Swindon UK.

[38.] Environment Agency' Evidence Directorate and Defra Flood and Coastal Erosion Risk Management Research and Development Programme 2011 Project: SCV060064/TR2 Design sea levels.

Morecambe Bay was formed during the Last Ice Age, 20,000 years ago and covers an area of 310 sq. km and has a 'funnel' shape with an uneven seabed which produces strong turbulent currents. At the entrance of this estuary is the Lune Deep approx., 20 km long this deep-water canyon has turbulent currents, cliffs and above intertidal mudflats punctuated by deep depressions. In extreme conditions the high amplitude of sequential wave 'trains' over the hollows, depressions and depths means the waves break at different times from vortices created by *singularities* in the water – i.e. vortices created by the force of the water against the seabed (100 tons/$^2$m of force). This force is funnelled up the Lune Deep which changes from approx., 1.066800m (3.5ft) shallow mudflats to approx., 46.02480m (151ft) and this depth has an impact on the violence of the waves in severe storm surge conditions. During normal storms' it is recognized that the 'sound comes from the oscillations of air bubbles' (discussion with Prof. McIntyre, DAMTP, University of Cambridge). Severe storm surge conditions accentuate the violence of the vortices created from singularities reaching the surface with unusual breaking waves clashing (clapping) furiously against one another as the currents flow back on themselves on the water surface. Therefore, the greater the force, i.e. the amount of water funnelled into the Bay, the higher the amplitude of the *turbulent* waves, these different surface noises derive from initially the severely uneven sea bed of the Lune Deep and the shallow and deep-water depressions of the mud-banks creating friction these underwater forces during severe storms contribute to this violent *turbulence*. It is this *turbulence*, not speed that generates the noise from surface waves which crash back into themselves from reverse currents hitting the inflowing currents of breaking wave 'trains'. As the depth of the bathymetry decreases the violence of the *turbulence* intensifies. When the depth increases, the *turbulence* diminishes. This depth alteration of turbulent water surface energy is translated into sound energy when the surface vortices hit the many sudden alternating depths and haloclines, reverse currents and thermoclines of 'wind driven' cold seawater hitting warm freshwater generating unusual breaking waves. Energy has to go somewhere – it is dissipated into sound energy as this is a surface manifestation. Turbulent surge conditions with the different viscosity of large saline inflow and fresh water outflow from rivers coupled with an offshore wind arise and affect the turbulence of the water surface when there is atmospheric pressure - a cyclonic low explained by G. W. Lennon[39]. The residual difference (known as a Skew Surge) between the predicted astronomical high tide and the nearest experienced high water is considerable; strong winds combined with these 'tidal outfalls' create short wave periods with steep furious waves noisily clashing from all directions. The height of the waves depends on the duration and strength of the wind and the noise is created from the inside of the breaking waves.

I submit that this is in part some of the sound, the *'on dyngesmere' - the sea of noise."* All are defined by the Admiralty RN Nautical Almanac Office; the Environment Agency[40]; and by J. Wolf[41]. Can wind speed be the other factor that determines the accentuation of the sound?

[39] Lennon, Geoffrey W. 1963 *The identification of weather conditions associated with the generation of major storm surges along the west coast of the British Isles.* Q.J.R. Meteorol. Soc., 89, 381-394.

[40] Admiralty RN Nautical Almanac Office 2012; the Environment Agency 2011 *Coastal Flood Boundary Conditions for UK mainland and islands Project: SC060064/TR2.*

[41] Wolf, Judith 2009 *Coastal Flooding: Impacts of coupled wave-surge-tide models.* Nat. Hazards 49, 241-260.

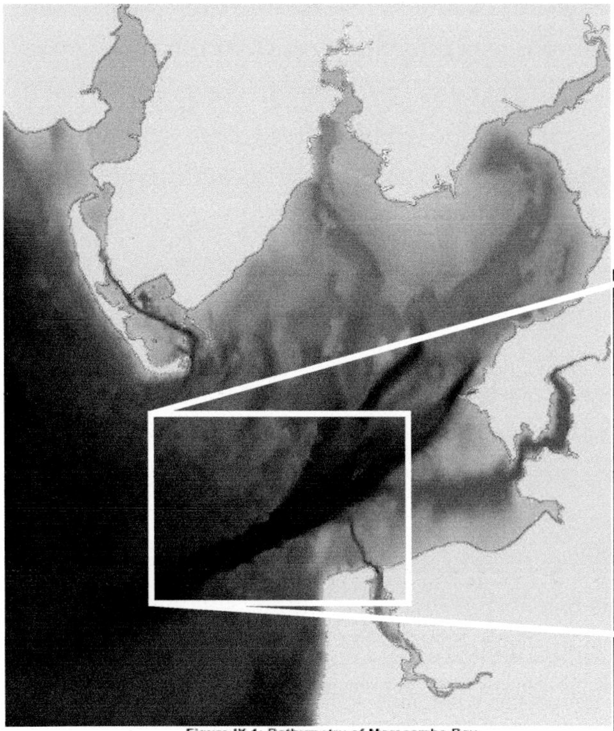

It is believed the Lune Deep was the original outlet for the five rivers flowing from glaciers before the sea rise after the Last Ice Age. (1845 The Civil Engineer and Architect's Journal (Nov), London, William Laxton, p337).

**Figure 6.** Analysis[42] Permission granted 22nd Sept 2016

**Figure 7.** Natural England [43] Note should be taken of the seabed. https://youtu.be/GSt9MWhe_HE (0.55) 17th May 2010. Credit: © Natural England (granted 20th Sept 2016)

**The fourth point:** we have discussed tidal disposition data of severe storm surges, and turbulence properties of the seabed bathymetry and now we must introduce other factors into the equation, acoustics and atmospherics – very low frequency (VLF) of the wind field. Some of the work that has been completed on this subject by Yang & Kwang 1997[44]; H.N. Oguz 1994[45]; Hamson 1985[46], is of importance. J.H. Wilson[47] (1979:1499) states,

"Measurement of ambient noise for very low frequencies (VLF) from 5 to 50 Hz indicate that wind generated noise is a significant source of the total ambient noise field during high-wind/sea-state conditions. Determining dominant physical mechanism(s) for transfer of energy from the wind field into the underwater acoustic field is very important in modelling the wind-generated noise field at very low frequencies. Frequency dependence, wind speed dependence directivity characteristics, and dependence on oceanographic parameters of the wind-generated noise source can be established only after the physical mechanism is understood."

---

[42.] Mason, D. C., Amin, M., Davenport, I. J., Flather, R. A., Robinson, G. J., Smith, J. A., 1999. *Measurement of Recent Intertidal Sediment Transport in Morecambe Bay using the Waterline Method.* Estuarine, Coastal & Shelf Science 49, 427-456.

[43.] Natural England, CC: https://youtu.be/GSt9MWhe_HE (0.55) 17th May 2010

[44.] Yang T.C., Kwang Yoo 1997 *"Modeling the environment influence on the vertical directionality of ambient noise in shallow water"* [J. Acoust. Soc. Am., Vol. 101(5), pp. 2541–2554].

[45.] Oguz H.N. 1994 *"A theoretical study of low-frequency oceanic ambient noise."* [J. Acoust. Soc. Am., Vol. 95 (4), pp. 1895–1912].

[46.] Hamson R.M. 1985 *"The theoretical response of vertical and horizontal line arrays to wind induced noise in shallow water"* [J. Acoust. Soc. Am. Vol. 78(5), pp.1702–1709]

Wilson (1979) identifies three physical mechanisms:
1. Interacting gravity and capillary waves.
2. Turbulent pressure fluctuations in the atmosphere near the ocean surface.
3. Oceanic/wave turbulence.

Wilson acknowledges the initial theory of turbulent pressure fluctuations initiated by M.A. Isakovich and B.F. Kur'yanov (1970:49-58)[48]. However, his emphasis is on the underwater acoustic properties for the transfer of energy from the wind field into the underwater acoustic field but the wind generated noise field exists on the surface as well and interacts as a two-way phenomenon of the wave turbulence with the sound energy and is clearly heard above the water surface. Wilson added the wave height spectra of Mitsuyasu and Honda (1974:29-42)[49] which he incorporated into the theory, since this is the accepted wave height spectra in the VLF acoustic region. This was unavailable at the time for M.A. Isakovich and B.F. Kur'yanov. When the wind blows over a wave surface, there are turbulent fluctuations in the pressure and wind velocity near the ocean's surface. Wilson's analysis of wind/wave data have shown the following basic features of the atmospheric turbulence near the ocean's surface:

(1). Turbulent pressure fluctuations in the atmosphere are strongly correlated with the wave height spectra and wind speed in the storm area.

(2). Wind speed and turbulent pressure fluctuations vary logarithmically with height above mean sea level with the lowest wind speeds and largest pressure fluctuations occurring at the ocean's surface.

Therefore, 'transmission of atmospheric sound (Dera 1992)[50] through a medium (of air and water), the sound intensity level interchanges with acoustic pressure level and are expressed in decibels,'

$$J = 10 \log \frac{I}{I_o} = 20 \log \frac{P}{P_o}$$

An important paper written by Zygmunt Klusekl and Aliaksandr Lisimenka 2013 p810 cites Makris and Wilson 2008 who state,

"A key problem concerning atmosphere-ocean interaction is mass exchange. The results of numerous experiments and theoretical models have revealed that the gas transfer rate depends on the entrained bubble concentration. It was subsequently found that passive acoustic techniques would be useful for evaluating gas exchange between sea and the atmosphere."

---

[47.] J.H. Wilson 1979 *"Very low frequency (VLF) wind-generated noise produced by turbulent pressure fluctuations in the atmosphere near the ocean surface,"* [J. Acoust. Soc. Am. Vol. 66(5) Nov, pp.1499].

[48.] M.A.Isakovich & B.F.Kur'yanov 1970 *"Theory of Low Frequency Noise in the Ocean,"* Soy. Phys. Acoust. **16**, pp. 49-58.

[49.] H. Mitsuyasu & T. Honda 1974 *"The High-Frequency Spectrum of Wind-Generated Waves,"* J. Oceanogr. Soc. Jpn. **30**, 29-42.

[50.] J. Dera 1992 demonstrates a number of formulae showing sound in and out of water. The above formula is accentuated by the severe weather conditions, high winds, tidal surges at the equinox, thermoclines and tidal outfalls, with the force of the water entering Morecambe Bay during a Low Pressure System.

Klusekl and Lisimenka (2013 p811) comment on work by Loewen and Melville (1991) who,

"Showed in their wave channel experiment that the energy of noise is well correlated with the wave energy dissipated as a result of breaking and stated that a significant part of the dissipated energy was consumed in thrusting the air bubbles downwards.".........." in view of the observed relationship between the energy of the noise produced and the dissipated mechanical energy of the breaking wave, it was suggested that the dissipation of wind wave energy in the Ocean should be estimated by means of ambient sea noise measurements."

They point out that there are a number of important factors,
- i) The shore zone showed that there are distinct differences in the character of noise spectra for different types of wave breaking....the slope of the noise spectra highlights plunging and spilling waves.
- ii) That investigations by Kennedy (1992) and Ding & Farmer (1993) were conducted under more realistic conditions.
- iii) Kolaini (1998) documented a 3-4 dB increase in the noise pressure level from the bubble cloud in salt water compared to the similar breaking process in fresh water.
- iv) Orris & Nicholas (2000) established that identical jets of fresh and salt water impinging perpendicularly on a water surface emit noise with different spectral-energy characteristics.

This last point is exactly the same as the confluence of various river waters mixing with saline water during the equinox tides in extreme weather conditions over the Lune Deep in Morecambe Bay. Independently of Morecambe Bay it has been observed by Klusek and Jakacki (1997) that a bubble cloud penetrated to a depth of 10m after a similar measurement of breaking wave height. (See page 11 Prof. McIntyre, DAMTP, University of Cambridge).

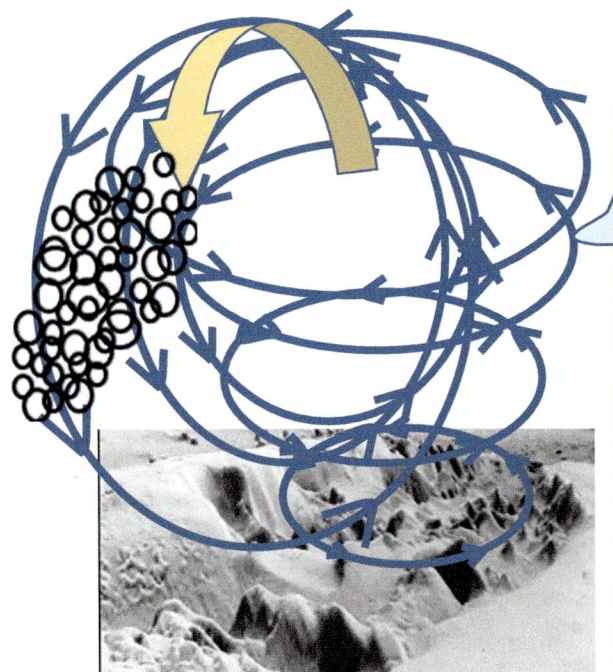

**Figure 8.** Action of vortices created from singularities on the seabed from the force of the inflow and outflow currents during extreme conditions; the breaking wave causing the bubble cloud through to a depth of 10m +. The important aspect is to remember the action of the wind factor on the breaking wave. Klusekl & Lisimenka 2013 state,

The potential energy $E_p$ of a wave train in the wave channel at position $x_i$ can be expressed as follows:

$$E_p(x_i) = \frac{1}{2}\rho_w g L C_g(x_i) \int_\tau \varsigma^2(t)dt, \quad (1)$$

where $\rho_w$ – water density, $g$ – acceleration due to gravity, $C_g$ – group velocity of a wave packet, $L$ – channel width, $\tau$ – integration time chosen on the basis of the wave packet persistence (limited to the time during which regular surface wave phase changes were being observed), $\varsigma$ – water surface elevation recorded at the wave staff.

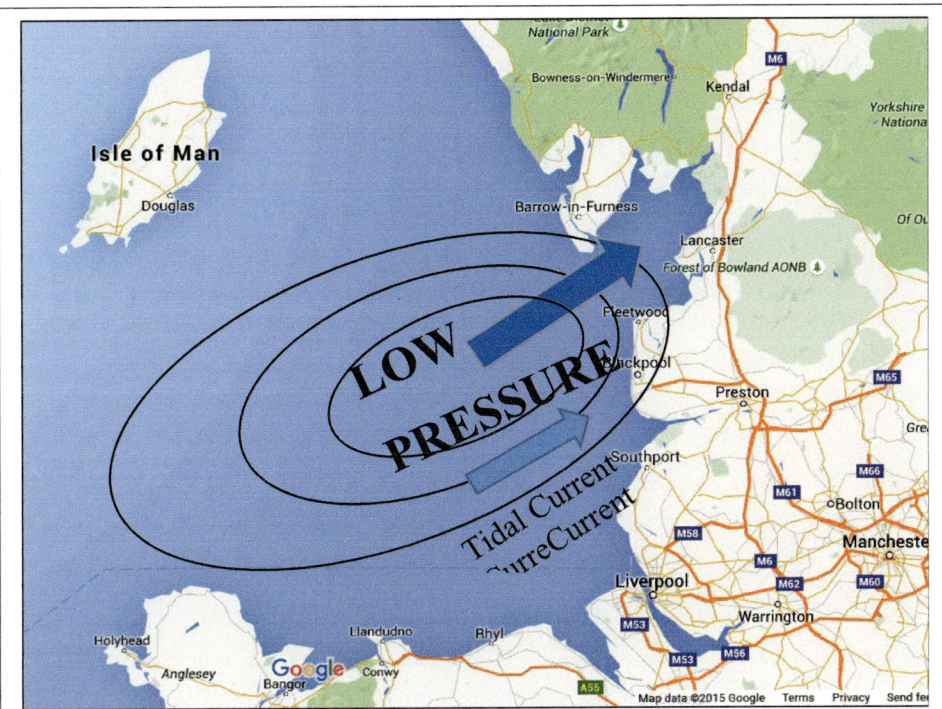

**Figure 9.** Irish Sea with Lancashire coastline highlighting Cyclonic Low Pressure in Morecambe Bay and Amounderness. (*Google Maps 2015*).

The sounds of the 'sea of noise' were similar to the 'battle sounds' over and probably on the mere (Bay) where the fleeing forces would be trapped and clearly *ón dyngesmere* became an iconic kenning [a type of trope - Gk. τροπος (*tropos*) – turn, direction, way; see the verb: τρετπειν (*trepein*) – to turn, to direct, to alter, to change], for those who fought at the battle. The cyclonic low pressure coming in from the south-west (Atlantic incursions) coupled with a cold front from the east creates heavy rain in the autumn months and a severe storm surges, conditions necessary for this noise. Could the projected scientific data interpreted by the NASA database be confirmed when compared to historical and landscape sources?

## COMPARISON OF HISTORICAL ANNALS WITH METEOROLOGICAL CONDITIONS

**The fifth point:** when this scientific data, compiled by the RN Hydrographic Office, is compared to historical record: i.e. the Annals of Inisfallen[51] (AD 937) which states: "A mighty wind" for that year, occurred at the equinox, it emphasizes the exact adverse weather conditions for a severe storm surge. Crucially, the weather conditions implied in the Anglo-Saxon Chronicles[52] for the years AD 935-940 are similarly bad, a cyclonic low pressure which pushes water into Morecambe Bay above 100 tons /$^2$m of force (see Dia.4, above). Both scientific projection together with historical weather evidence match and confirm the conditions. Gradually deposited silt created a low estuarine area with uneven depressions in Morecambe Bay, as the rise in sea levels occurred this geological aspect created a funnel effect. These maritime events - surges and bores up the rivers Leven and Kent, change the bathymetry and resonances in extreme turbulent conditions, when the equinox occurs each year in March and September. For these reasons the shifting sands plus mudflats are hazardous.

---

[51.] *Annals of Inisfallen* highlight this climatic event of high winds and high tide at the autumn equinox surge combined with the turbulence from the Lune Deep and Tidal Outflows creates the unique conditions for this noise.

[52.] G.N. Garmonsway 1965 *Anglo-Saxon Chronicles* Dent and Son.

| Month | Jan | Feb | Mar | Apr | May | Jun | Jul | Aug | Sep | Oct | Nov | Dec | Year |
|---|---|---|---|---|---|---|---|---|---|---|---|---|---|
| Average high °C | 6.8 | 7.1 | 9.1 | 11.6 | 15.2 | 17.3 | 19.4 | 19.4 | 17 | 13.7 | 9.8 | 7.6 | 12.9 |
| (°F) | -44.2 | -44.8 | -48.4 | -53 | -59.4 | -63.1 | -66.9 | -67 | -63 | -57 | -49.6 | -45.7 | -55.2 |
| Average low °C | 1.7 | 1.6 | 3.1 | 4.2 | 6.9 | 10 | 12.4 | 12.3 | 10.2 | 7.3 | 4.3 | 2.5 | 6.4 |
| (°F) | -35.1 | -34.9 | -37.6 | -40 | -44.4 | -50 | -54.3 | -54 | -50 | -45 | -39.7 | -36.5 | -43.5 |
| Average rainfall mm (inches) | 81.1 | 58.7 | 68.3 | 48.9 | 49 | 59.8 | 59.5 | 73.4 | 82.5 | 97.9 | 94 | 58.3 | 871.3 |

Climate data for Blackpool (1971–2000 averages)

**Figure 10.** Climate data for Blackpool. CC Source: the Met Office

Contemporary Climate Data for the Blackpool area demonstrates that the wettest months for this area are September, October and November at the time of the autumn equinox. It supports continuous historic climatic changes plus maritime evidence in the panegyric which can be verified and cross referenced to historical annals. Notably: *ofer æra gebland*, (over the sea-surge) **qualifies the type** of feature that would **create the physical aspect** *ón fealene flod* (on the dusky flood tide/the fallow flood) the outcome being the **transient sound** *ón dyngesmere* (on the sea of noise); all highlight a unique feature, a distinctive natural event on the sea that would be well known to people in the locality. Consequently, *ón dyngesmere* the 'sea of noise' **is a valid and tangible reality.** This 'unique sea of noise,' the *ón dyngesmere* of the *Brúnanburh* poem, is supported by these natural climatic events. The intention of scientific analysis to describe the historical MS does not diminish its value, rather I submit it is expressly effective at identifying the location of events.

## NEW EVIDENCE - THE FYLDE ARGUMENT

**These above five points are prerequisites** and bring us to the Fylde argument. For if the maritime couplets and their scientific investigation, when compared to historical analysis, were the only type of evidence found in the *Brúnanburh* poem, then they could easily be dismissed as coincidence. Other aspects corroborate this view and robustly reinforce this argument: that Amounderness was where the battle(s) took place. Amounderness, known as the Fylde, was derived from the Old English *gefylde* – the district of the plain[53]. Moreover, this word is employed in surrogate phrases used in the *Brúnanburh* poem. On this coast was a Northumbrian PN: Burn Naze, described as *Brúne Næs* in the Domesday Book, around which there was a series of muddy creeks on the flat coastal area near Thornton and Poulton le Fylde. Interestingly, Burn Naze (*Brúne Næs* is Pre-Domesday[54] dating from around AD 700) an early Anglian harbour; the derivation of this Anglian word *Brúne - gives chronological credibility.* What is the cartographic evidence to support such an argument?

**LANDSCAPE ANALYSIS.** The phrase *'manuscript evidence is material culture'* supports the Fylde argument against all other lines of reasoning. Landscape analysis employing early cartographic analysis reveals an area of creeks around this place-name on the Fleetwood peninsula. In AD 937, the creeks would be most prominent as modern drainage schemes were non-existent but what attracted my attention from this cartographic analysis was a specific place name (PN) – OE *Bergerode in* exactly the same place as Burn Naze!

[53.] See Ekwall 1922 p.139. Also, Garmonsway 1965 *Anglo-Saxon Chronicles* Dent and Sons.

[54.] Ekwall 1922 *Place names of Lancashire.* Manchester University Press, p.157.

Significantly, the poem states **'ymbe Bru<sup>n</sup>nanburh**[55] - **around Brúnanburh**, noticeably not 'at Brúnanburh, and this aspect becomes crucial showing both the encircling quality of a fortified area. *Burn/Brúne Naze* in *Bergerode* is on raised ground called a (O.N.) *'holmr'* surrounded by creeks. John Porter's analysis in 1876[56] of Burn Naze appears to have been overlooked by scholars: it offered a protective harbour not only from the sea surges but a position that would be easily fortified with stakes and an earth wall barrier.

Topographically, before Sir Peter Fleetwood gave his name to this peninsula in 1800-10 this area was called *Bergerode* (see Figure 11 and 12, below). The prefix of *Bergerode* appears to be developed from A.Sax. *beorg*, *berg* a protection, refuge derived from the verb *beorgan* (i) to save protect, shelter, defend, fortify spare, preserve. (ii) to defend, secure; A.Sax. *Ród*, *rode* refers to - a measure of land, a clearing[57]. The first word of *Brúne Næs* may be derived from the A.Sax. *brún*; adj. Brown, dark, dusky; *Sió brúne ýþ* – the dusky wave/billows, found in Boethius Met. Fox, Metrum XXVI 58 p.335[58]. Naze is derived from O.E. *næs* meaning headland. Below Burn Naze is Trunnah – O.E. *trun* round and O.E. *hóh*, a burial mound, Porter (1876) concurs about mounds.

**Figure 11. 1577** Saxton, Christopher. *Lancastriae comitatus palatinus*. (Facsimile, in B32, Map Chest 3 – Sheet Map5eqd72.F). (*Permission of Lancaster University 2015*). http://libweb.lancs.ac.uk/maps/map2H1693.jpg

**Figure 12. 1753** (Map 4A) Morden, Robert. 'The County Palatine of Lancaster' (1695) final state of Morden's large map from Camden's *Britannia* (London, 1753). (*Permission of Lancaster University 2015*). http://libweb.lancs.ac.uk/maps/map4A1753.jpg

---

[55.] G.N. Garmonsway 1965 *Anglo-Saxon Chronicles* Dent and Sons. See also Heale Grandon 2006 *'Fylde and Wyre Antiquarian Society'* (March). See Bosworth and Toller Main Vol. *'yumbe'* p1295.

[56.] Notice should be taken of Porter's work which has long since been forgotten but is quite correct and clearly demonstrates the 'pad's' and the burial mounds.

[57.] Bosworth & Toller revised Toller 1898, *Anglo Saxon Dictionary*. O.U.P. The age of the word *Bergerode* is peculiarly Anglo-Saxon, even though the earliest mention to be found so far is 16th century; also Burn Naze is found in the Domesday Book as *Brúne Naes*.

[58.] See Rev. Samuel Fox (trans) of King Alfred's *De consolatione philosophiae by Anicius Manlius Severinus Boethius* Metrum XXVI 58 p335.

Also the battle took place near a prominent hill. Such a hill exists to the south west of Burn Naze at Warbreck ON: *varði, varða* 'beacon' a ridge over 100ft high and ON: *brekka* 'slope' defined in 1922 by Ekwall[59]. The author found confirmation for *Bergerode* with the specific maps of Christopher Saxton (1577; see Figure 11), William Hole (1607), John Speed (1610), Richard Blome (1717) and Robert Morden in (1753; see Figure 12), all verify and illustrate the original OE name of the peninsula. They identify the area of *Burn Naze* clearly as *Bergerode* - fort clearing. While the cartographic evidence is sixteenth century; this does not diminish the OE words *Brúne* and *Bergerode,* highlighting again chronological credibility. Thus, the author suggests that *Brúne Berg* may be the origin of the name as the prefix of *Brúnanburh* and word *Brúne* are identical, rather than *Brome* of Bromborough.

Germane to this robust argument are two interesting facets of evidence which can be confirmed by archaeology. Although there is some dispute about the two causeways – Danes Pad and Kates Pad, specific evidence has been found, but logically there must have been paths/causeways from Burn Naze, Skippool and the Roman Port of *Portus Setantiorum* mentioned by Ptolemy which curved southward to Kirkham and joined a Roman Road. The first piece of evidence is a Romano-British route called *Danes Pad* (an anomaly in a settlement area of Hiberno-Norse) from Preston across to Burn Naze and Skippool Creek, harbours dating from the Anglo-Saxon and Viking Age (see Figure 13, below). These harbours would be required to berth a large amount of longships carrying an army of warriors and provisions, for the draught of a longship was approximately 1 metre enabling access to the creeks. The second piece of evidence is *Kate's Pad* across Pilling Mere (Pill – a saltwater creek into which freshwater drains). In 1975 F. T. Wainwright[60] drew attention to this other Romano-British causeway most probably a corruption of the Brythonic *Catt* = battle, hence 'battle path'.

This may have relevance to the transient sound (*dingesmere*), the 'clashing' mere represented in the poem, the turbulent storm representing the swords and vice versa. Also J. Porter raised the issue of burial mounds found along both *Pads.* Secondly, the area south of the river Lune is described as the Fylde, derived from O.E. *-gēfylde*: *gē* 'district' and O.E. *-feld*, Mod. Eng. *fylde* 'plain'- the district of the plain,[61] known also as Amounderness. The pertinent words in the poem are, *feld dæn$^n$ede, ón wælfelda* (the plain of the slain) mentioned in lines 12 & 52 of the *Brúnanburh* poem. However, thirdly, *Stede* (estate) is mentioned three times. *Campstede* "the place of battle" or "battle estate" is specified twice in lines 30 & 50; also, *ón folcstede* "on the country dwelling of the folk" or "rural estate" in line 42. Account should be taken of these aspects as *Brúnanburh* is only mentioned once. Landscape analysis of words in the poem pinpoint this region: **Feld/Fylde** and an estate (the **stede** of the place-name (PN) Treales Old Welsh *Tref-llys* - the palace of the country folk (***folcstede***).

---

[59.] Ekwall 1922 *Place names of Lancashire*. Manchester University Press.

[60.] Wainwright, Frederick T. 1975 *Scandinavian England*. Ed. H.P.R. Finberg. Philimore. As well as these two causeways or pads Wainwright describes Ingimund's invasion of the Wirral in AD 902 which would account for the number of Scandinavian-Irish names.

[61.] Bosworth & Toller revised Toller 1898, *Anglo Saxon Dictionary*. O.U.P.

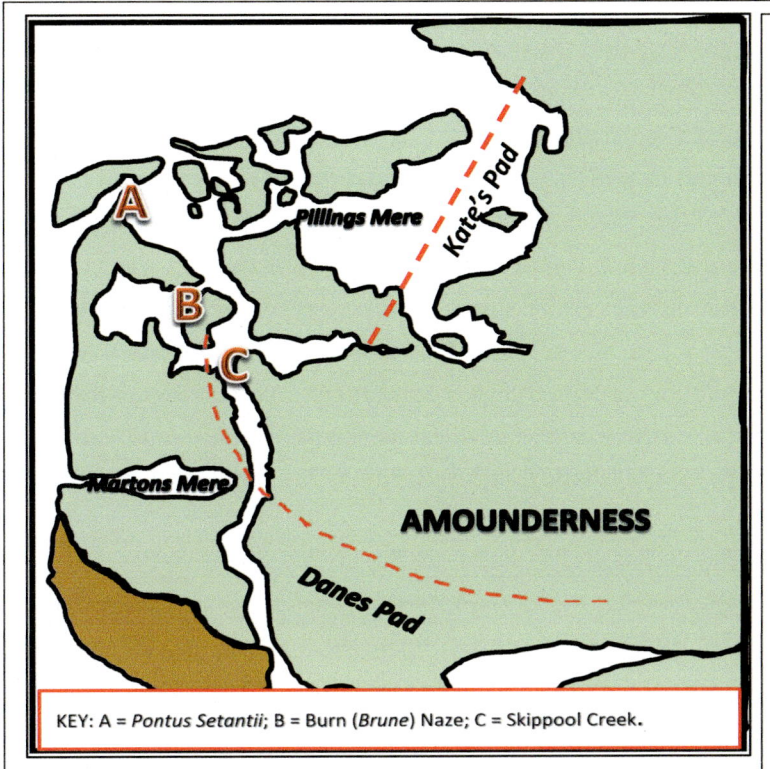

**Figure 13.** Base map the *'Fylde and Wyre Antiquarian Society'* assessment (after work of *Grandon Heale March 2006*)[62] to illustrate the many creeks and the coastline. This was before the silting up of these channels. The draught of the longboats would have to be shallow enough in order to navigate these creeks (the longboats had a draught of one metre). Such an area would accommodate more than 150-200 + longboats. The curved line from Fulwood Moor north of Preston is *Danes Pad* a footpath to Skippool Creek and to Burn Naze. (Noticeably, Burn Naze sits on a raised area of land). The peninsula was anciently called *Bergerode* and its prominence on all maps suggest an ancient origin. The line over Pillings Mere is *Kate's Pad* i.e. Brythonic *Catt* = Battle, therefore Battle Path. *(Digitally drawn by J.R. Kirby 2015)*.

KEY: A = *Pontus Setantii*; B = Burn (*Brune*) Naze; C = Skippool Creek.

**Figure 14.** A distance of one mile separates Treales and Lund (© *Ordinance Survey of Great Britain New Popular Edition No.94 Preston 1945 1:63360*)[63]. CC granted 22nd Sept 2016, www.visionofbritain.org.uk Ekwall (1922 pp152 and 150)[64] states of Kirkham Parish **Treales** - Court of the settlement or palace; **Lund** - grove respectively. Notice most particularly a 'Watling Street', derived from O.E. **wealhas** - foreigner.

---

[62.] Heale Grandon 2006 *'Fylde and Wyre Antiquarian Society'* (March). I am indebted to the Fylde and Wyre Archaeology Group for much investigation on the causeways and identifying the creeks.

[63.] *Ordinance Survey of Great Britain New Popular Edition No.94 Preston 1945,1:63360* www.visionofbritain.org.uk

[64.] Ekwall 1922 *Place names of Lancashire*. Manchester University Press, p.150 p.152.

Fellows-Jensen (1991:77-96)[65] highlights the habitative generic O.Welsh: '*Tref-*'(n), "The **only PN containing '*tref*'** to be found between 'Triermain' in Cumberland and the many in Wales is 'Treales' in Lancashire." The importance of 'Treales' (PIE: *treb*; O.Irish: *treb*; OE: *ðorp* - home village) is implied as two field-names use the Roman word *Chester* indicating the status of this PN. Stretching across towards Fulwood Moor we are able see a PN called 'Lund' – a grove, (in the church of which there is a Roman altar) and to determine that within the Roseacre and Wharles parish took place *the initial battle* and then *the later battle* around (*ymbe*) Burn Naze (*Brúne Næs* DB) which is in keeping with the movement of the two armies in the poem. For according to the poem Æthelstan split the two armies – the Hiberno-Norse (Irish Gaelic: *Gall-Ghaedheil* - foreign Heathen Gaels) were pursued to the ships along Danes Pad and the surviving Scots with the Strathclyde Welsh going north along Kate's Pad to escape the fierce battle. As sound travels' faster over water than land, the investigation of north Lancashire and south west Yorkshire has proved fruitful. This argument speaks for itself: we do not need to 'fit' a PN based on similarity to the name *Brúnanburh* as the Fylde argument stands on merit.

These topographic points reinforce Amounderness as the general locale through research into specific maritime words plus phrases mentioned in the poem and has identified this approximate locale. Underlining this as an absolute is the aerial photograph (see Figure 2, p.9) of the surge occurring at the Walney Meetings. This aerial photograph demonstrates beyond doubt the evidence of a surge still occurring today. When one experiences the turbulent force of the surge by standing on the Vickers Bridge the sound and power is considerable. This loud sound occurs when the water passes over the stony Chapel Beds and under the Vickers Bridge to the stony area to the east of the Furness peninsula. The main audible characteristic is a resounding low rumbling sound (VLF) primarily caused during severe surge sea conditions at the equinox coming from Morecambe Bay, Celt: *combe*. Noticeably, this physical backdrop, amplifies the sound which may be heard for miles, hence this kenning *dingesmere*. Although Wood (2013 p149) maintains *Anlaf/ Óláfr* "came to York with a large fleet .... the passage eastwards through the Pentland Firth is an easy sail in the summer" this cannot be the correct analysis. *Anlaf/ Óláfr* was fighting in Ireland (see p.12) in the summer (Annals of the Four Masters) coupled with the High Winds (Annals of Innisfalen) the Humber landing is immediately ruled out. Subsequently the direct route from Dublin to York via Amounderness would be the area that *Anlaf* would choose and want to control.

### FIELD-NAMES ON AMOUNDERNESS - THE BATTLE ON THE PLAIN

What is not appreciated is that the Battle consisted of two phases (according to the poem in the Anglo-Saxon Chronicles). The first battle was on the plain (the Fylde) around Treales, Lund, Deepdale Wood and in the Roseacre and Wharles Parish with initial skirmishes on Fulwood Moor. Various words in the poem state, *ón folcstede* "on the country dwelling of the folk" and the *Campstede* "the place of battle" or "battle estate" – there is only one prominent ancient estate on the Fylde i.e. (Treales). Notice the coaxial fields established by the Romans[66] but above Lund there is an open moor later divided during the enclosures.

---

[65.] Gillian Fellows-Jensen 1991 *Scandinavians in Dumfriesshire and Galloway: the place-name evidence.* pp77- 96, in *Celtic Norse Relationships in the Irish Sea in the Middle Ages 800-1200.* Eds Jón Viðar Sigurðsson and Timothy Bolton, Brill, Leiden 2014.

**Figure 15.** Field System between Kirkham, Treales and Lund. Notice Anglo-Saxon Tenement Strips and areas of Moor. Teales fields has two named *Chester* and there is the Roman Altar in Lund Church. However, the initial battle was probably fought across this area and beyond Deepdale Wood. (*Nat. Archives Kew - Tithe Map IR30/18/311(Treales 1839), IR30/18/79(Kirkham & Lund 1840). Digitally drawn by J. R. Kirby. 2017*).

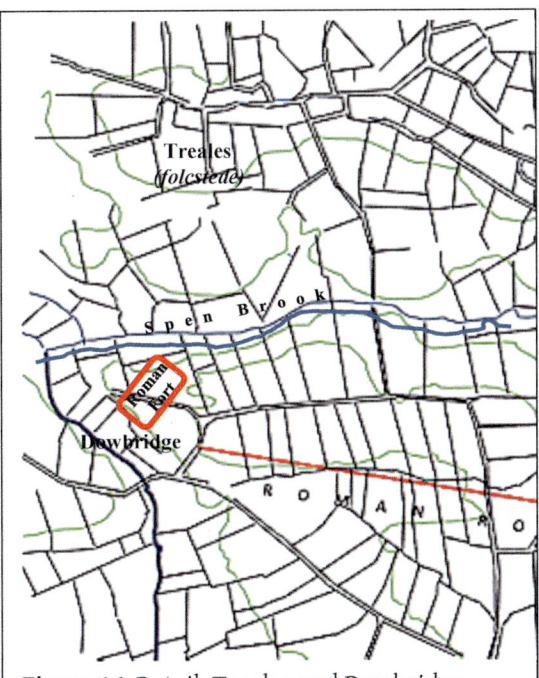

**Figure 16.** Detail. Treales and Dowbridge Area. The Roman Fort at Dowbridge is to the north of the road later known as Danes Pad.

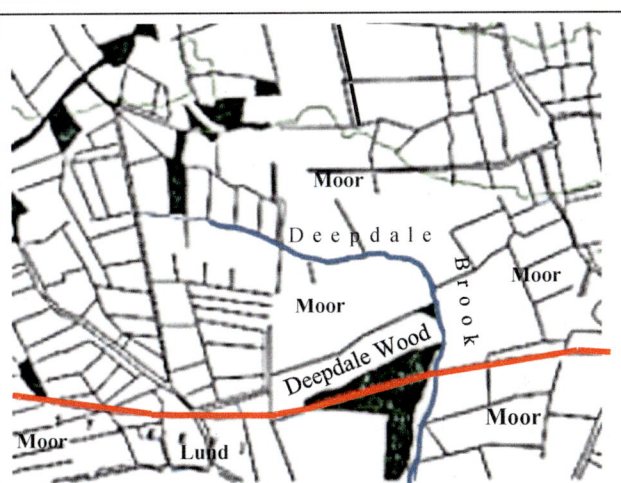

**Figure 17.** Detail. Deepdale Wood and the Moor a continuation of Fulwood Moor north of Preston. The Roman road, known as 'Watling Street', was derived from OE: **wealhas** - foreigner and passes across the Deepdale Brook through Deepdale Wood in the direction of Lund to Kirkham. To the North of Deepdale Wood is the Moor.

[66.] Coaxial field systems are also known as *Centuriation,* which was a method of land measurement – a regular layout based on a square grid using surveying instruments such as the *Groma* –surveying straight lines and right angles; *Chorobates* – horizontal planes; *Dioptra* for levels, angles of slopes – modern version is a theodolite. [67.]

Key for sources: WW- W. Wainwright, EE -Eilert Ekwall, B&T – Bosworth & Toller, C.V.C – Cleasby, Vigfusson & Craigie, R&S - Rivet & Smith.

# FIELD-NAMES AROUND *TREALES & LUNDR* - THE FIRST BATTLE.

***Treales*** Kew, Nat. Arch. Sept 2017 - IR 30/18/311 Tithe map of Treales, Roseacre & Wharles; IR 29/18/311 (Apportionments).

**Treales** – Village Name: Welsh. *Tref-llys*, the site or town of a hall, court or palace. [EE; WW].
**06a.088 Gill Holme** – ON: *gil* ravine, narrow valley with a stream at the bottom. [C.V.C.; WW].
**22.544 Ray Holme** – ON: *vrá* corner. [C.V.C.; WW].
**09.252 Whinny Nook** – (Scand. origin) *Whin* furze, gorse. Prob. related to Norwegian *kvein*. [WW];
        More prob., OIc: *Kveina* – to whine, to cry, to wail, mourn, lament. [C.V.C.].
**22.367 Balm Brig Meadow** – ON: *bryggia*, bridge; cf. OE: *brycg*.
**08.157 Chester Field** - Roman: *castrum* – a military camp or fort. [R&S]; an old fortification. [K.C].
**07.091 Broscow Meadow** – ON: *skógr* – wood. [C.V.C.; EE; WW].
**20.226 Tarn Hey** – ON: *tiǫrn*, tarn. [WW].
**Spen Brook** – River name - ME: *spen*, *spenne* prob. of Scandinavian origin. OIc: *Spenna* grasp, to draw
        as in *spenna boga* to draw a bow. Possibly ref., to the 'width' of the brook. [C.V.C.; WW].
**06a.088 Spend Meadow** – the grasping/drawing meadow.
**13.027 Goody Butts** – ME: *Butte* applied to a strip of land abutting a boundary.
**07.261 Great Silly Nook** – ME: *nook* – a corner.
**06a.254 Three Nooked** – ME: *nook* – a corner, *three nooked* - triangular piece of land.
**06a.513 Parrock** - OE: *pearroc*, a small enclosure. [WW].


*Roseacre and Wharles*

**Roseacre** – Village Name: ON: *hreysi* - field with a cairn, a heap of stones [EE]. 'They probably indicate the existence of a stone circle or burial mound'. [WW].
**30. 989 Wharles Acre** – OE: *hywrfel*, ON: *hvirfill* – a circle, ring. [WW].
**34.995 Wharles Acre** – OE: *hywrfel*, ON: *hvirfill* – a circle, ring. [WW].
**38.865 Croneberry Field** – derived from Old Saxon 8th century – 12th century **cwáne** - to lament, bewail,
        deplore or mourn but is also found in OScot: *Crone* – wail, lament, mourn;
        -berry, -bury, *byrig* – stronghold, OE: <u>*beorġe*</u>. ME: *Bergh*.
**38.859 Croneberry Field** - the bewailing burgh field; *field* – open piece of land [K.C.].
**30.864 Cronebury Field** - the bewailing burgh field; *field* – open piece of land [K.C.].
**12.447 Croneberry Hey** - the bewailing burgh; *hey* – enclosed piece of land [K.C.].
**31.726 Small Tail** - OE: *tægl*, *tægel*, [B&T]. ME: *taile* – a tail (a piece of land jutting out from a
        larger piece. [WW].
    **Mote Field** – poss. OE: *(ge)mot* – a 'moot' or meeting place [WW].
**34.667 Ranget** – ON: *vrangr* - crooked, twisted [C.V.C.], < OE: *wrang*. [WW].
    **Northaws** – North ON: *haugr* - hill, barrow [WW].
    **Long Shoot** – OE: *sceat* – a division of a field [WW].

### *Newton with Scales (plus Lund)* IR30/18/229(Map) IR 29/18/229(Apportionments)

- **01.392 Stonebrigg Carr** – OIc: *Bryggja* – a gangway, bridge, landing stage, [C.V.C.]. British: **briua* – bridge [R&S]; OIc: *Kjarr* (Dan: *Kjær*) - copsewood, brushwood, *kjarr-mýrr* - marsh overgrown with brushwood. [C.V.C.]
- **08.107 Crooklands** – ON: *krókr* – a hook, a barb on a spear or arrow, anything crooked. [C.V.C.; WW]. OIc: *Land* – land; compounds *landa-mæri* – border-land, *landa-merki* a landmark, boundary of an estate [C.V.C.]; Hooked Land poss. Inversion compound.
- **10.204/5 Evenham** – ME: < *avenam, ofnam* < ON: *afnám* – same as *intack*, a piece of land cut off or enclosed from a larger piece.[WW]
- **09.135 Carr Gate** – ON: *kiarr* (ME: *kerr,car*, ModE: *carr*) used for low lying ground, ON: *Gata* road. [WW].
- **Lund** – Village Name: OIc: *Lundr* – a grove [C.V.C.].
- **05.100 Scale Moor / Scale Meadow / Scale Croft** – ME: *scale* < ON: *skali* – hut. [WW].
- **02.043 Brockholes Hey** – OE: *brocc* – badger, hence badgerhole. [WW].
- **03.372 Grippool** – *Grip* - a ditch, channel or furrow for drainage. [WW] *Pool* – an area of water.
- **07.122 Parrock** – OE: *pearroc*, a small enclosure.[B&T;WW].
- **04.027 Small Tail** – OE: *tægl, tægel*, [B&T]. M.E. *taile* – a tail (a piece of land jutting out from a larger piece.[WW].
- **05.954 Syke** – ON: *sík*, OE: *sīc* – a small stream in marshy ground (rare prob. of Scand. origin).[WW].
- **12.228 Wheel Meadow** - OE: *hywrfel*, ON: *hvirfill* – a circle, ring. 'There are five grouped together indicating they existed before the division of the large field and are of ancient origin'.[WW].
- **05.100 Scale Moor** –ME: *scale* < ON: *skáli* – hut.

### *Clifton with Salwick* IR29/18/79(Map) IR30/18/79(Apportionments)

- **22.715 Cringle Syke** – ON: *Kringla* – circle; ON: *sík*, OE: *sīc* – small stream in marshy ground (prob. of Scand. origin). [WW].
- **24.699 Crook** – ON: *Krókr* – corner, crook, nook. [C.V.C; WW].
- **08.104 Drawmire Dale** - ON: *Mýrr* – a mire, swamp. [WW].
- **20.606 Sour Field** – ON: *saurr* – mud. [C.V.C.; WW].
- **04.681 Wham** – ON: *Hvammr* – hollow. [C.V.C; WW].
- **04.241 Fog Field** – ME: *fogge* – aftermath, long coarse grass (prob. of Scand. origin). [WW].
- **20.727 Higher Gill** – ON: *gil* - ravine, narrow valley with a stream at the bottom. [C.V.C.; WW].
- **18.546 Lund Syke** – ON: *lundr* – a grove. [C.V.C.; WW].
- **04.678 Dipdale Wood** - Deepdale Wood
- **08.178 Barrow Dales** – dales with tumuli on them.
- **21.790 Ramm** – prob. Derived from *Whamm* (ON: *Hvammr*, hollow). [C.V.C.; WW].
- **11.307 Woe Meadow** – OE: *wóh* - twisted, wicked.
- **26.532 Lund Chapel** ON: *lundr* – a grove. [C.V.C.; WW].
- **13.315 White Field** – ON: *Hviti* – white.

Both the initial battle and the secondary battle occurred during the course of a day. *"All through the day"*. From the analysis of the battle site locales, two unusual field-names are conspicuous when assessments are made for 'strongholds' in both areas: Roseacre and Wharles Parish plus Burn Naze in Thornton Parish. They are:-

**Croneberry Field** and **Cronebury Field** – O.Scot. *Crone* – wail, lament, mourn; -berry, -bury, *byrig* – stronghold; OE: <u>*beorġe*</u>. ME: *Bergh*. Wright (1898: 804a)[68] states, Crone refers to cranberries or whortleberries (*Vaccinium Oxycoccos*) but the origin of this name is considerably older than Old Scottish and was used at the time of the Battle derived from Old Saxon, 8th century to 12th century ***cwáne*** to lament, bewail, deplore or mourn – Mid Eng: *Croyne*, M.Low Germ: *Kronen* – to moan, groan, lament. [See *Scottish National Dictionary*[69]] The introduction of 'cranberry' was phonetically late medieval circa 1560, and noticeably no cranberries are to be found. Reinforcing the OE argument, it is also seen in general colloq. use as the groaning of an old woman OE: ***ealdcwén*** - an old crone.

The same seems to have applied to **Borty Berry** but in a slightly different way. Wright (1898: 360b-361a) notices a dialect term which refers to the **Bour tree** - OSc, Irel, Lancs, Nhb, Cumb, Wm, Yks, – elder tree (*Sambucus Nigra*) ASax: *Aeld* meaning fire, but it was thought this name was medieval circa 1450 and disguises a possible name in OScot. Brockie 1886:114[70], describes an interesting folklaw, "bur-tre or bore tree is supposed to possess great virtue in guarding against the malevolence of witches, fairies etc." As such it may well have been placed on top of the stronghold to cleanse it of incantations and previous divinations. Mention of this particular plant (name) giving protection is found in the Guisborough Cartulary (1199-1203)[71] – *Buirtrekelde* (elder-tree well). The fact that the suffix **berry/bury,** in the Northern dialect, of both *Croneberry* and *Borty Berry* are peculiarly indicative of strongholds reinforces the ASax./OScot., line of reasoning in both cases. In addition, the virtue in guarding against the malevolence of witches, fairies the name *Bortyberry* is also found in Ireland where the Norse Heathen had come from and was used to purify areas from spells, divinations, ritual and Heathen incantations.

The Pre-Christian belief in Gaelic/Celtic tree worship highlighted the 'elder' as a vegetation goddess who echoed the rhythm of the waxing and waning of the moon. While the prefix of the former field name **Croneberry Field** refers to a physical event of great lamentation, the latter **Borty Berry** implies a superstitious cum religious event. Essentially this battle highlights a fundamental paradigm: establishing Christian Laws for good governance over unbridled Heathen powers of suspect origin. This gave *Æthelstan* a national mandate and international credibility.

[68] Wright, Joseph. 1898 *The English Dialect Dictionary: being the complete vocabulary of all dialect words still in use or known to have been in use during the last two hundred years*. 804a

[69] *Scottish National Dictionary* (eds) William Grant (1929-1946) and David Murison (1946-1976).

[70] Brockie, William. 1886 *Legends and Superstitions in the County of Durham*.114.

[71] Cottonian Manuscript Cleopatra d ii (British Library). Ed by W. Brown and published by the Surtees Society from 1889

## FIELD-NAMES OF *BERGERODE/BRÚNE* - THE SECOND & FINAL BATTLE.

Above the river Ribble, the Jarldom of Amounderness was part of the kingdom of Northumbria; the field-names of Trunnah and Burne (*Brúne*) on the *Bergerode* peninsula expose the second battle. They reveal imprints on the landscape of ancient structures and Saxon 'tenement strips.'(Kew, National Archives July 2017 - IR 30/18/303 Tithe map of Thornton, by Thomas Hull 1839). IR29/18/303 Apportionments. [Key: First two numbers denote each sheet; last three numbers are the apportioned field numbers].

**18.440** Garlick's Hey – (*North. dial.*) Simpleton; Hey – enclosed piece of land (OE: (*ge*)*hæg*). [B&T].

**21.368** Field Side – The field on the east side of Trunnah fields, a part of Trunnah fields.

**19.379** Trunnah Field – (*North. dial.*) round barrow/burial.

**14.372** Trunnah Field – (*North. dial.*) round barrow/burial.

**14.376** Town Field – apportioned to the town, village orig., (*North. dial.*) round barrow/burial.

**19.377** Top Trunnah Field – (*North. dial.*) round barrow/burial.

**16.420** Marsh Field – Land with wet soil which was subject to flooding and useless for growing crops, however it was valuable as grazing land in the summer months. Marsh could also be called moor as it was not fit for ploughing.

**27.241** Intack – (*North. dial.*) A piece of land taken in from a moorland, common; an enclosure.

**21.335** Hulls Lower Arley – ASax: *Ár-léas* (masc. nom.) – dishonourable, impious, wicked, cruel. ASax: *Ár-léas* datable to between 8$^{th}$ and 10$^{th}$ century [B&T].

**19.365** Tinkler's Hey – Where itinerant travellers camped (?).

**19.364** Farther Railway Field – industrial revolution period.

**03.655** Lagran Meadow – ON: *Lög-rán* - Legally seized property. [C.V.C].

**11.557** Lagran – ON: *Lög-rán* - Legally seized property. [C.V.C].

**12.555** Lagran – ON: *Lög-rán* - Legally seized property. [C.V.C].

**12.558** Long Lagran – ON: *Lög-rán* - Legally seized property. [C.V.C].

**14.300** Sandyforth Nook – (*North. dial. & Scand.*) Nook. An outside corner of a building or any upright structure; the corner of a street. Now *rare*.

**21.316** Creek – Area of incoming seawater meeting outflowing freshwater continually flooding.

**28.315** Red Marsh – ON: *Rauðr* - red. The river Wyre colour is a dark reddish brown. [C.V.C].

**21.339** Arley – ASax: *Ár-léas* (masc. nom.) – dishonourable, impious, wicked, cruel. [B&T].

**21.317** Hulls Arley – ASax: *Ár-léas* (masc. nom.) – dishonourable, impious, wicked, cruel. [B&T].

**21.341** Hulls Arley – ASax: *Ár-léas* (masc. nom.) – dishonourable, impious, wicked, cruel. [B&T].

**21.340** Hulls Arley – ASax: *Ár-léas* (masc. nom.) – dishonourable, impious, wicked, cruel. [B&T].

**21.336** Hulls Arley – ASax: *Ár-léas* (masc. nom.) – dishonourable, impious, wicked, cruel. [B&T].

**21.335** Hulls Lower Arley – ASax: *Ár-léas* (masc. nom.) – dishonourable, impious, wicked, cruel. [B&T].

**21.356** Marks Arley – ASax: *Ár-léas* (masc. nom.) – dishonourable, impious, wicked, cruel. [B&T].

**21.351** Bottom Arley – ASax: *Ár-léas* (masc. nom.) – dishonourable, impious, wicked, cruel. [B&T].

**21.352** Bottom Arley – ASax: *Ár-léas* (masc. nom.) – dishonourable, impious, wicked, cruel. [B&T].

**21.346** Castle Field – Known as Castle Hill – a Bryth/Scand, later Saxon (?) fortified earthworks.[WW].

**21.342** Wallets – OE: *weall* meaning wall or ME: dialectal form of *welle* meaning stream.

**21.345** Nearer Knep – ON:/ OIc: *kneppa* - studded, [C.V.C]. OE: *cnæpp*, ON: *knappr* - hillocks.

**21.145** Old Kneps – ON:/ OIc: *kneppa* - studded, [C.V.C]. OE: *cnæpp*, ON: *knappr* - hillocks.

**07.491** Stana Kneps – (*North. dial.*) Bumpy Stoney Ground (Poss. Burial area); – ON:/ OIc: *kneppa* - studded, [C.V.C]. OE: *cnæpp*, ON: *knappr* - hillocks.

21.147 **Staina Dales** – (*North. dial.*) Bumpy Stoney Ground (Poss. Burial area); Scand. *Deill* a share of land in a common field (rare); Poss: *Steinn* personal name.

28.001 **Angersholme** – OE: *anger* – Pasture identical with German *anger* – meadow, on the ON: *holme* – Island [EE].

21.148 **Little Burtyberry** – (*North. dial.*) berry - a burgh, an ancient fortified settlement. Borty – elder berry or Northern dialect for 'old' burgh.

21.151 **Great Burtyberry** – (*North. dial.*) berry - a burgh, an ancient fortified settlement. Borty – elder berry or Northern dialect for 'old' burgh. See Roseberry Topping Northumberland. [EE].

28.153 **Burty Berry** - Ditto

28.154 **Burty Berry** – Ditto

28.155 **Burty Berry** - Ditto

18.121 **Borty Berry** – Ditto

18.156 **Borty Berry** - Ditto

18.157 **Borty Berry** – Ditto

18.160 **Borty Berry** - Ditto

Key for sources: [B&T] Bosworth and Toller; [C.V.C] Cleasby Vigfusson and Craigie; [EE] Eilert Ekwall; [K.C.] Kenneth Cameron; [WW] F.T. Wainwright.

18.120 **Bottom Barty Berry** - (*North. dial.*) berry - a burgh, an ancient fortified settlement.

**Butts Lane** – *Butts* - a raised boundary, an embankment; the lane surrounds the Fields.

24.100 **Biggins Field** – ON: *byggja* – a dwelling, to settle as a coloniser. [C.V.C].

22.122 **Old Earth** – (uncommon name) original old ploughed land.

18.125 **Old Earth** – (uncommon name) original old ploughed land.

22.133 **Green Dicks Hey** – Green Dykes, Drains; *Hey* – enclosed piece of land (OE: (*ge*) *hæg*). [B&T].

22.134 **Hook** – OE: *hōc* - a corner, a bend.

22.127 **Cleves** – OE: *clif*, cliff. [B&T].

18.128 **Cleves** – OE: *clif*, cliff. [B&T].

18.130 **Cleves** – OE: *clif*, cliff. [B&T].

21.348 **Crib Field** – OE: *crib(b)* (fem) A barred receptacle for fodder used in cowsheds and fold-yards; also in fields, for beasts lying out during the winter. [B&T].

21.355 **Field Behind Crib** - OE: *crib(b)* (fem) an area where the bodies were lain after the battle.(?)

19.282 **Nearer Stanny Furlong** - ASax: - stony (metalled) street.

19.281 **Further Stanny Furlong** - ASax: - stony (metalled) street.

28.181 **Stanny Furlong** - ASax: - stony (metalled) street.

22.182 **Stanny Furlong** - ASax: - stony (metalled) street.

22.183 **Stanny Furlong** - ASax: - stony (metalled) street.

23.215 **Barn Field** – site of an ancient barn.

23.193 **Old Landed Field** – original land / settlement.

22.191 **Great Holmes Croft** – OIc: *Hólmr* – islet, esp. in a bay, creek, river; even meadows on the shore with ditches behind them are in Icelandic called *Hólmr* [C.V.C].

26.058 **Rytherham Field** – OE: *hrȳðer* – ox; second element is ON: *holmr* island not OE: *ham*. [EE].

26.057 **Rytherham Field** – OE: *hrȳðer* – ox; second element is ON: *holmr* island not OE: *ham*. [EE].

18.141 **Stalmines Kneps** – First element – OE: *stell* stream, brook; second element ON: *mynni* mouth of a brook, or river [EE]. (*North. dial.*) Bumpy Stoney Ground (Poss. Burial area); – ON:/ OIc: *kneppa* - studded, [C.V.C]. OE: *cnæpp*, ON: *knappr* - hillocks.

Geographically, there were a number of islands (*Hólmr*) in those ancient times that were surrounded by marsh and creeks. The *Hólmr* have been identified (below in green). Also, the field system consists of examples of Anglo-Saxon 'tenement strips' indicating the age of these fields.

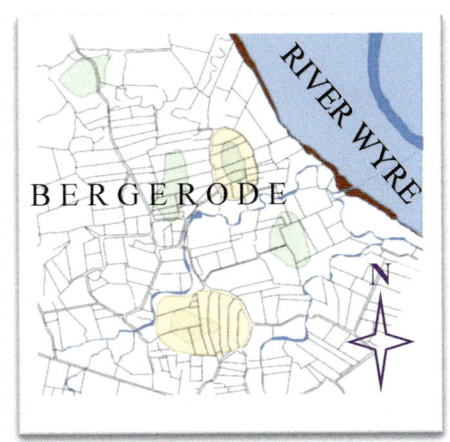

**Figure 18.** Tithe Map of Thornton by Thomas Hull 1839. Notice the closeness of the River to the burgh and its defensive placement with two large streams to the south of the burgh. (*Nat. Archives Kew IR30/18/303. Digitally drawn by J. R. Kirby 2017*).

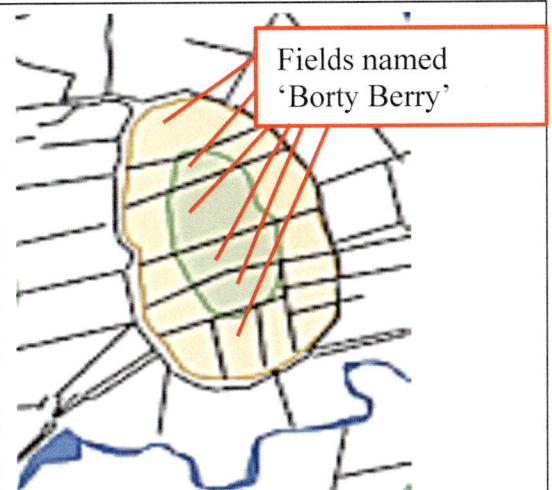

**Figure 19.** Detail of Tithe Map. Yellow area = bounds of shape which may constitute a burgh. Green area = raised ground constitutes a *Hólmr*.

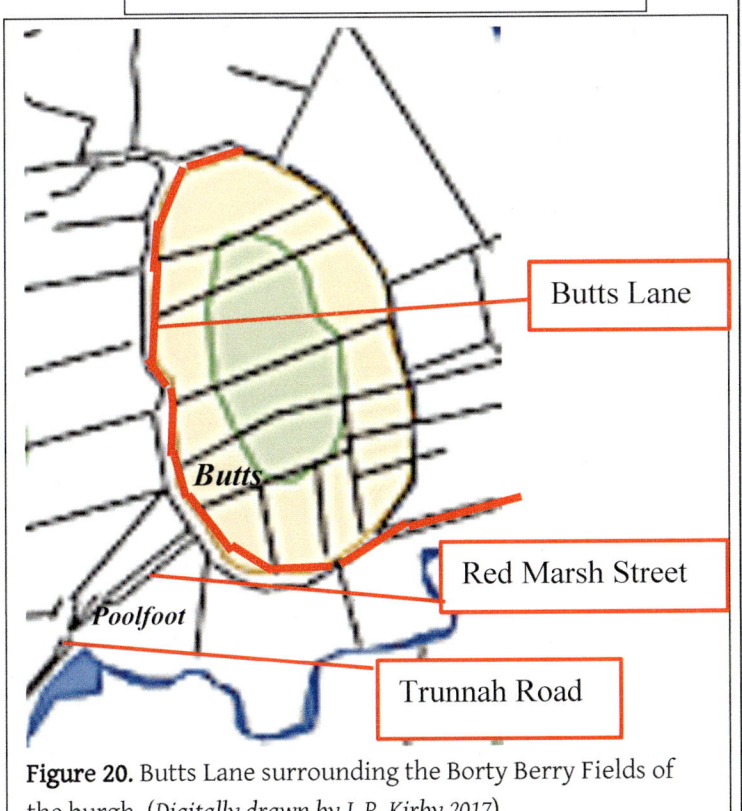

**Figure 20.** Butts Lane surrounding the Borty Berry Fields of the burgh. (*Digitally drawn by J. R. Kirby 2017*).

The use of the field-name 'Borty Berry' [also 'Barty,' 'Burty,'] (*North. dial.*) a *burgh*, an ancient fortified settlement, repeated six times, all next to one another, are extraordinary and extremely rare. They demonstrate the peculiar bounds of each field encompassing a circular shape. This circular form must have been substantial to survive all these centuries and still be showing this demarcation. The bank or rampart (was probably topped by a wooden stockade) of the hedge forming this shape would have contain a ditch and a 'berm' (a ledge between the scarp and the exterior slope of the rampart). This ditch/berm and rampart is much flattened now worn down to a slope, yet still runs alongside Butts Lane, the continuation of the Trunnah Road that branches north called Hey Street, then to Red Marsh Street and finally into Butts Lane (*butt* – denoted a strip abutting on a boundary, a short strip or a ridge). Butts Lane (in Red opposite) still defines this shape.

Beyond, this feature south of these peculiar field shapes are larger fields called 'arley' ASax: *Ár-léas* (*masc. nom.*) – void of honour, shameful, infamous, impious, wicked, or cruel. These unusual field-names are clearly Anglo-Saxon denoting the 'age of their naming'. Both 'arley' and 'borty berry' fields lie close to one another. [The author notes that the antonym to 'impious' is 'pious' which is exactly the state of Æthelstan's devout character and his expectation of his warriors].

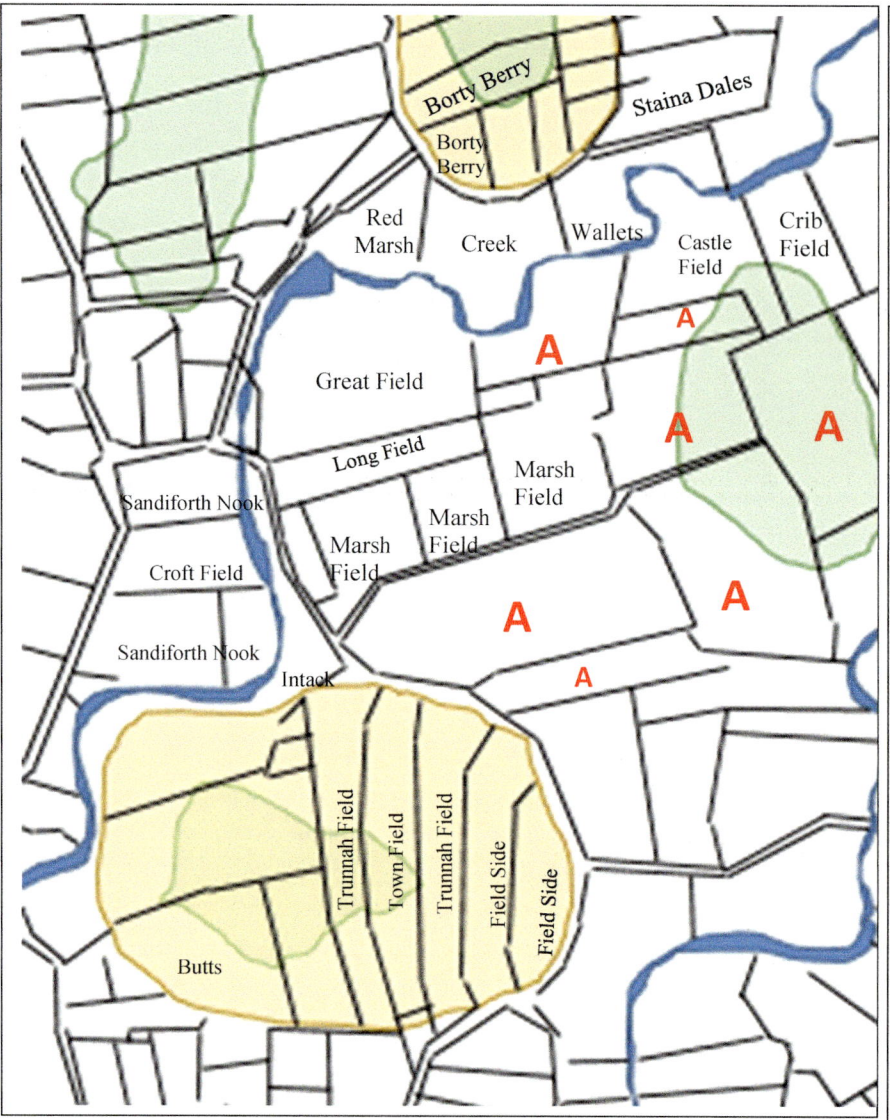

**Figure 21.** Field-names between *Trunnah Fields* and *Borty Berry Fields*. Notice the **A** symbol of peculiar field names called 'arley' *(Anglo-Saxon) Ár-léas* (masc. nom.) meaning dishonourable, impious, wicked, or cruel. It is not only the names of these fields on the *Bergerode* peninsula which suggest this was the *Brúne around the Burgh*, the *Borty Berry Fields;* (see Eilert Ekwall – Roseberry Topping) but also they have become such robust statements of evidence that suggest this was the site of the last battle, the *Brúnanburh*. The *Annales Cambriae* 1860 Ed. Rev. John Williams Ab Ithel, p17, describe the battle as "*Bellum Brune*".[72] It is also their strategic position that is significant. Because of the *Marsh Fields* the direction of attack would follow the better ground of the *Arley Fields*, appropriately named, around and across the stream into *Staina Dales* and the *burgh*. (Digitally drawn by J. R. Kirby 2017).

Strategically, I suggest that the area with the field-name 'arley' ASax: *Ár-léas* may be to 'cover' the retreating Heathen forces; to hold the might of Æthelstan's advancing forces before reaching the burgh. Noticeably, surrounding the 'Borty Berry' area on the southern side from Poolfoot to Holme Pool is a substantial stream leading to the river Wyre. This stream flows into another called Hillylaid Pool again leading to Holme Pool, both streams making a considerable obstacle for an opposing army to overcome. Further, the lie of the land of the eastern side from the 'Borty Berry' fields' slopes down to the river Wyre allowing easy access to any longships berthed there. Between these two streams there are interestingly named fields called Trunnah fields - a name referring in *North. dial.* - round barrow/burial. These independent pieces of landscape evidence are not coincidence for they form a forceful argument for the true site and are therefore datable to the time of the last battle around *Brúnanburh*.

[72.] The *Annales Cambriae* 1860 Ed. Rev. John Williams Ab Ithel, p17.

## SOCIO-POLITICS IN THE NORTH-WEST

Socio-politically *Æthelstan* had bought the area of Amounderness on 7th June 934, the equivalent of a jarldom; he gave it to the Archbishop of York, *Wulfstan I*, if he could hold onto it (Charter S407). This was three years before the battle. It is mentioned in historic Charters recorded by W. Farrer in 1914[73], by Sawyer in 1968[74] and again by C. Hart 1975[75]. (see Whitelock, D. (ed.) 1955 No. 104, in answer to the argument that this charter was spurious). Historians have given the scribe who wrote *King Æthelstan's* charters in a hermeneutic style, between AD 928 – 935 as "Æthelstan A". He uses the title *Rex Britannia* and he may have been a Mercian. *Jarl Þurferth* (ODan: *Þurfrith*, ON: *Þórrøðr*, AngloDan: *Thored*) who was Jarl of Northampton in the Danelaw (AD 916-934) was placed in charge of this area by *Æthelstan* and *Archbishop Wulfstan I*[76]. Unfortunately, *Jarl Þurferth* was killed later that year AD 934 on *Æthelstan's* Scottish Invasion, probably near Abercorn, or on the moor of Fortriu. The appointment of *Þurferth* to a jarldom in Southern Northumbria by *Wulfstan I* was a shrewd move as *Þurferth* would be regarded as 'a lawful certainty,' his ancestors and kin had settled in the Furness area since AD 830[77]. He was a 'known person' to the Christian community, plus this move cut off the direct route to York from Dublin. Wood (2013) has confused 'Southern Northumbria' with 'the south of York. Politically this (S407) was the best strategic move that *Æthelstan* could make as a devout Christian king by stopping the Heathen faction from abrogating Christian law, gaining territory and influence the northern peoples. However, *Æthelstan's* territorial expansion interfered with the political aspirations of the Scots and the Welsh kingdom of Strathclyde-Rheged, hence their involvement in the conflict. As Jarl of Northampton *Þurferth / Þórrøðr* had submitted to Edward the Elder in AD 917[78] (Garmonsway 1965, 1975) because the Heathen Norseman *Ragnall* invaded the North of England. *Jarl Þurferth Thoruson* and his family were of ancient Danish origin and had been Christians since AD 826[79] (ARF) as such he kept his jarldom under the suzerainty of *Æthelstan the Half-King* of East Anglia. *Jarl Þurferth* was married to *Hlífr* daughter of *Jarl Tørf Einar Rognvaldsson* of the Orkneys and *Queen Þurriðr*, the widow of *King Þursteinnr Rauðr*. *Þursteinnr* (ComScand./ODanish) had originally settled in the Furness area before moving to the north of Scotland (cf. Orkneyinga Saga[80], Landnámabók[81]).

---

[73]. Farrer. W. (ed) 1914 *Early Yorkshire Charters.* Vol 1, Edinburgh. Highlights the area allotted to Wulfstan of York who placed *Þurferth* in charge though there is every reason to suggest that *Þurferth* expanded this area.

[74]. Sawyer. P.H. 1968 *Anglo-Saxon Charters. An Annotated List and Bibliography.* Royal Historical Society Guides and Handbooks, 8 London No.520. See Charter S407 at Nottingham in AD 934. (See S416 & S425 Jarls of the Danelaw).

[75]. Hart. C. 1975 *The Early Charters of Northern England and the North Midlands.* Leicester. Chapter VII 117.

[76]. This was Æthelstan's 'modus operandi' to place the church in overall charge of areas to bring Christianity to those areas and exclude Heathenism. See Kirby, J.R. *Egil's Saga: Traditional evidence for Brúnanburh compared to Literary, Historic and Archaeological Analyses* for *Þurferth/Þórrøðr's* origins and his son *Jarl Gunnar* who fought at Brunanburh.

[77]. Kirby J. R. 2013 *Early Settlements and their related vills on the Furness peninsula - Dalton parish c. AD 800-1200.* Unpublished Post Graduate Dissertation in Archaeology, University of Oxford. (See Field-Names).

[78]. Garmonsway 1965, 1975 *Anglo-Saxon Chronicles.* See year AD 917. Poetically, the two words **dynge** and **ding(e)** [see page 6] would be portraying the **mere** as a 'trapping area' like a dungeon and the noise of the turbulent incoming sea over shallow mudbanks plus deep depressions would be descriptive of a complex 'kenning'.

[79]. Annals Regni Francorum. See G.H. Pertzii and Fridericus Kurze 1895 *Annals Regni Francorum. inde AB A. 741 usque AD A. 829 qui dicuntur Annals Laurissenses Maiores et Einhardi.* Hannoverae, pp. 169-170.

[80]. Orkneyinga Saga. See Paul Edwards tr. with Hermann Pálsson 1978 London: Hogarth Press.

[81]. Landnámabók. See Guðbrand Vigfússon and F. York Powell. 1905 *Origines Islandicae.* Vol 1, Oxford.

Þurferth is *Com.Scand./O.Danish* but Þórrøðr is *O.Norse*, indicating a linguistic change that occurred between AD 870 to AD 900, but this change would have occurred later in the Danelaw. [Whitelock(1940:78-80) cites von Feilitzen (1937) and states, "It is a normal anglicizing of ON: i.e. *Guðrøðr*, a later form of ON *Guðfrøðr*, O.Dan. *Guthfrith*, AngloDan. *Guthferth, Gudrod*" – highlighting a linguistic change with this type of name].

**Figure 22.** Line of Anglo-Saxon forts blocking the Scottish and Northern Welsh armies from fleeing north. Bromborough could **not** be the site of the battle of *Brúnanburh* for this very reason. These forts existed before the reign of Æthelstan and formed part of Mercia. Also, it is noted that the Mercian frontier with Northumbria was at the Ribble. (*Imagery©2015 Getmapping plc, Infoterra LTD & Bluesky, Google, Bluesky, Digital Globe, Landsat, Data SIO, NOAA, U.S. Navy NGA, GEBCO. Map Data © 2015*

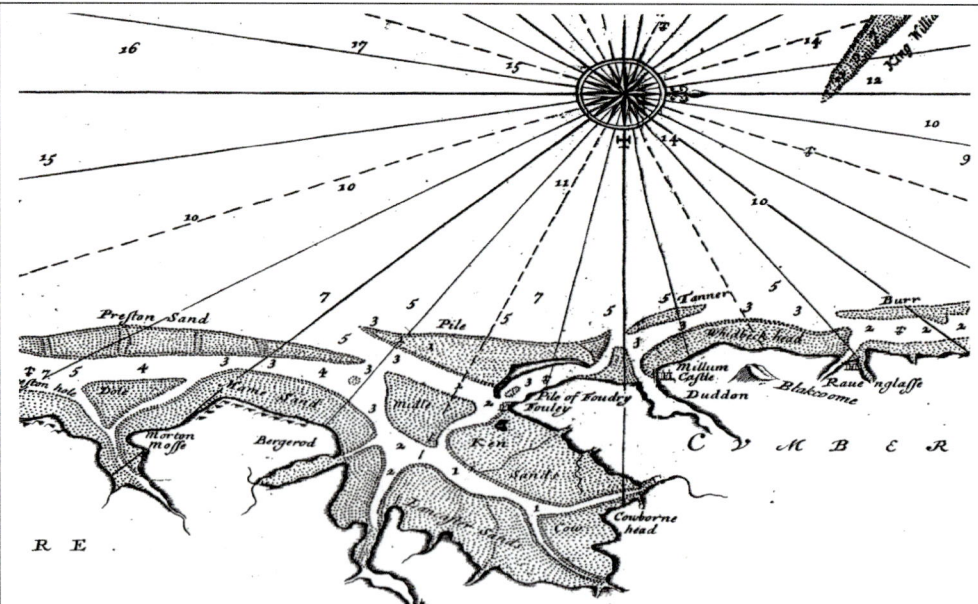

**Figure 23.** Note *Bergerod*. Image taken from "Great Britain's Coastal Pilot" produced by Captain Greenville Collins RN. Fylde Coast 1689. An early scientific approach which again bears out the early form of the name *Bergerode*. Notice the other peninsula's all have anciently derived names.

*Jarl Þurferth Thoruson's* son, *Jarl Gunnar Þórrøðrsson*, inherited the jarldom of Southern Northumbria and fought for *Æthelstan* at *Brúnanburh* leading the Christian men of the Danelaw into the battle. It was *Gunnar* who called the *Wapentake* – the weapon gathering, for his jarldom of Southern Northumbria was the one invaded. Tradition relates that the call/summons was 'hiere geleðian' to the west assemble! This was the primary law of the Danelaw, each jarl aiding the other i.e. the gathering of the Christian men of the Danelaw to the battle against the Heathen Norse. The threat and attack integrated those who were Christians in - the Danelaw, the Danes of York, the Northumbrians, the East Anglians, the Mercians and those of Wessex, all fought as one establishing the Nation State of England. Wood (2013 p 152)[82] maintains from two sources (Annals of Clonmacnoise[83] and the Chronicle of Henry of Huntingdon[84]) that *Anlaf/ Óláfr*,

> "Gave battle with the help of the Danes of that kingdom".... "augmented his army with
> ... Danes living in England. These can hardly be other than from Northumbria or the
> Five Boroughs, people like *Æthelstan's dux Urm* (of Leicester?), who according to a
> northern annal preserved by Roger of Wendover[85] was the key figure in winning the
> allegiance of the Five Boroughs in 940 for *Anlaf Guthfrithsson*".

This was clearly not AD 937 for "*Anlaf* married *Alditha* daughter *Earl Orm* by whose counsel and aid he had gained the victory aforesaid" (Roger of Wendover p251). Obviously, this must be the AD 940 invasion after *Æthelstan's* death, *dux Urm* supported the Heathen cause. This immediately brings into question the statement they "entered the mouth of the river Humber with a mighty fleet"; obviously, this was after AD 937 and plainly not the *Brúnanburh* campaign. Roger of Wendover continues, "*Æthelstan* compelled *Anlaf* and *Constantine* to take refuge in their ships". This last statement is in stark contrast to the *Brúnanburh* poem which states that *Constantine* fled overland to the North and *Anlaf* to his ships. From these statements Wood deduces, "That the Northumbrians submitted to the invaders in 937" (p152), implying that **all** the Northumbrians and the Five Boroughs supported *Anlaf*. Evidently, this is not so as the Christian *Jarl Gunnar Þórrøðrsson* of Southern Northumbria supported *Æthelstan* along with other Christian men of the Danelaw, for there was a distinct political difference inherent in both the Scandinavian society of Northumbria and the Danelaw. This difference was demonstrably between those who believed in Christianity and those who chose Heathenism. *Þórrøðr / Thored* was the eldest son of *Gunnar* and *Helga,* named after his dead grandfather - ODan: *Jarl Þurferth* (ON: *Þórrøðr,* later Anglo-Danish: *Thored*). *Þórrøðr* calls his eldest son *Jarl Æthelstan* (he is mentioned in his cousin's Will, *Prince Æthelstan,* of 1014, who was the elder brother to *Edmund Ironside). Jarl Æthelstan* was killed at Ringmere in 1010 fighting for the Royal Anglo-Saxon House. *Þórrøðr's* daughter was the first wife of *Æthelred II* and had both *Prince Æthelstan* and *Edmund Ironside* (*Ailred of Rievaulx, Twysden col 362, 372, EAF j687*)[86]. Further, before *Þórrøðr Gunnarsson* becomes Jarl of York he is recorded as wasting Westmorland and north Lancashire (AD 966 A.S.C).

[82] Wood, Michael 2013 *Searching for Brunanburh: the Yorkshire Context of the 'Great War' of 937*. Y. A. J. 85, pp138-59.

[83] *Annals of Clonmacnoise from the earliest period to AD 1408*(trans. AD 1627 by Conell Mageoghagan, ed. by Rev. Denis Murphy for the Royal society of Antiquaries of Ireland. Dublin, University Press. 1896, 154. (See AD 931 p150-1 for AD 937. The names of *Anlaf's* Captains who were killed at the battle are given in this extract.)

[84] *Chronicle of Henry of Huntingdon*, Trans. & Ed. Thomas Forester, (1853) London. Thomas Forester cites Brumby (after Ingram and Giles) in Lincolnshire near the river Trent. (See p.169 note 6; also the date is wrongly ascribed to AD 945 and should be corrected to AD 937).

[85] Roger of Wendover, *Flowers of History. The History of England from the descent of the Saxons to AD 1235 formerly ascribed to Matthew Paris.* Trans. By J.A. Giles Vol 1 (1849) London. (See p.251).

[86] Ailred of Rievaulx, (Ed.) Roger Twysden, *Historiae Anglicanie Scriptores X* (1652) col 362, 372, EAF j687.

## A DISCRETE APPROACH - DNA ANALYSIS

Harding (2004) tries to establish some sort of credibility by maintaining that the original Vikings who settled on the Wirral were 'R1b' haplogroup[87]. Recently Harding et al. (2008) has published in British Archaeology (No.103) an article about Viking DNA maintaining that the 'R1b' haplogroup was common to these earlier Vikings of the Wirral[88]. The 'R1b' Haplogroup is sometimes known as the 'Atlantic Modal STR Haplotype (AMH)' defined by 6 STRs [alleles](DYS 19, 388, 390, 391, 393, 394) – 14-12-24-11-13-13 covering 56% of western European R1b individuals (Wilson estab. 2001)[89] and this has been portrayed by some as the deciding group identifying Viking ancestry. Harding et al.(2008) states in his article that the 'R1b' halpogroup is the most common in Scandinavia and represents Scandinavian genes if found in peoples of the British Isles.

However, the R1b is the original haplotype for a Celtic not the Scandinavian population and the subclade R1b3 describes a version of that haplotype. The R1b haplotype is found as 30% in Norway (Faux 2008)[90]. Sykes (2006) states the phrase AMH (Atlantic Modal Haplotype) most probably refers to Celtic origin[91]. Yet the original stock of male Viking DNA appears to have been 'I1a' haplogroup. That is not to say that there were other haplogroups in Scandinavia but the major families, mentioned in this paper have been classified as 'I1a' haplogroup and this has been verified from the direct descendants. This can be seen from research produced by Agnar Helgason et al. (2001), mapping the whole of the Icelandic population of 'Y' chromosomes and as these remain constant the alleles or markers should clearly correspond[92].

The AMH type would appear to be Celtic and have spread from Spain after the last Post Glacial Maxim. They would have travelled up the Atlantic coastline by boat or into Britain across Doggerland, [which is now underwater i.e. the Dogger Bank], and into part of Denmark. In Tacitus's analysis of the tribes on the Danish peninsula we are faced with the *Cimbri*, who were probably Celtic - 'R' haplogroup, but they disappear as a group from history and are replaced by the Danes, Jutes, Angles and Goths.

According to current research (Balanovsky & Rootsi et al. Jan 2008[93]; see Semino & Passarino et al. 2000[94]; and Rosser & Zerjal et al. 2000[95]):-

---

[87] Harding, S., Cavill, P., Jesch, J. 2004 *Revisiting Dingesmere*. Journal of English Place Name Society, Vol 36, pp. 25-38.

[88] Harding, S., Jobling, M. 2008 *Vikings*. British Archaeology. (Nov-Dec), pp.22-25.

[89] Wilson J.F., et al. 2001 PNAS vol 98. No. 9, 5078-5083.

[90] Faux. David K. 2008 A Genetic Signal of Central European Celtic Ancestry: Preliminary Research Concerning Y-Chromosomal Marker U152 (Part 2) Hallstatt Culture: 720 BC to 600 BC and 600 BC to 480 BC (Ha C and D). http://www.davidkfaux.org/files/LaTene_Celt_R1b1c10_part2.pdf

[91] Sykes, B.C. 2006 Blood of the Isles. Bantam Press, A division of Transworld Publishing, Random House Group, London.

[92] Agnar Helgason et al. 2001 *mtDNA and the Islands of the North Atlantic: Estimating the Proportions of Norse and Gaelic Ancestry* Am. J. Hum. Genet. 68:723–737, 2001

[93] Balanovsky & Rootsi, et al *Two Sources of the Russian Patrilineal Heritage in Their Eurasian Context* Am J Hum Genet. 2008 Jan 10; 82(1): 236–250. Published online 2008 Jan 4.

[94] Semino,& Passarino et al. 2000 *The Genetic Legacy of Paleolithic Homo sapiens sapiens in Extant Europeans: A Y Chromosome Perspective*. Science. 10 Nov 2000:Vol. 290, Issue 5494, pp. 1155-1159.

[95] Rosser & Zerjal et al. 2000 *Y-Chromosomal Diversity in Europe Is Clinal and Influenced Primarily by Geography, Rather than by Language* "The American Journal of Human Genetics" Volume 67, Issue 6, December 2000, Pages 1526–1543.

"western Europeans carry predominantly haplogroup R1b, whereas eastern Europeans have high frequency of R1a lineages, that southern Slavs are characterized by high frequency of I1b, whereas Scandinavia is enriched with I1a."

Bryan Sykes (personal discussion 2006 at Wolfson College, Oxford), confirmed that the descendants of *King Þursteinnr Rauðr*, were 'I1a' haplogroup according to his research. Note also the focus of the 'I1a' haplogroup which is very pronounced and unique to Scandinavia. Therefore, R1b haplogroup can be seen to highlight a Celtic distribution because of its allele levels of AMH amongst Irish and Welsh individuals (see Sykes 2006).[96] R1a haplogroup analysis by Balanovsky & Rootsi et al. (2008) [97] seems to strongly confirm Baltic-Slav origin. However, the highest frequency Y haplogroup, according to geographical distribution, in Scandinavia is in fact the 'I1a' haplogroup. The Last Glacial Maxim (LGM) may have seen the movement of the 'I1a' haplogroup into Scandinavia as the ice sheet declined. This was enhanced during the Scandinavian Migration Age (c. AD 400 – c. AD 600), though because of their *Völkewanderung* from the Thrace area up to the Baltic some scholars maintain that they were as early as the Bronze Age. They are defined by the P19, M170, M258, P38, P212, U179 genetic markers with 40.3% prevalence in Norway; 42% in Sweden, 32% in Iceland and 35% in Denmark, but only 20% in Scotland, Wales and England. I1a has the specific alleles DYS19=14, DYS392=11 and DYS390=23.

Agnar Helgason, et al., (2000a[96] 2000b[97]) working for the company deCODE in their analysis mapping the Icelandic gene pool, their conclusion was that the 'I1a' haplogroup is the Scandinavian determinant whether a person might be of Viking (i.e. Scandinavian) origin. Genealogical analysis corroborates scientific DNA as comparison of historical research with this DNA analysis confirms the descendants of most of those families mentioned previously are of an I1a haplogroup. The above investigation by Balanovsky & Rootsi et al. (2008) [100] further confirms this analysis. In addition, this article raises concerns over the sampling of men with particular surnames by Harding and Jobling (2008 p23) [101] which give a false or skewed result. For example, the Kirby/Kirkby/Kirkeby name has 2 'Y' haplogroups, in general terms, one R1b the other I1a. Such 'Y' haplogroup duality within names indicates different origins. This paper suggests that if this is the norm for one name then other names must also be suspect. One cannot rely on a name to indicate only one 'Y' haplogroup without scientific analysis. Such research cannot be correct or academically proper to show even approximate results in this format; populist use of Personal-Names to 'secure' an analysis is regrettable. Greater rigor is required. Specific analysis is mandatory to assess each individual irrespective of the Personal-Name.

[95.] Rosser & Zerjal et al. 2000 *Y-Chromosomal Diversity in Europe Is Clinal and Influenced Primarily by Geography, Rather than by Language* "The American Journal of Human Genetics" Volume 67, Issue 6, December 2000, Pages 1526–1543.

[96.] Sykes 2006

[97.] Balanovsky & Rootsi et al. 2008

[98] Helgason, Agnar, Sigurðardóttir, S., Nicholson, J., Sykes, B., Hill, E., Bradley, D., Bosnes, V., Gulcher, J., Ward, R., and Stefánsson, K. 2000a *Estimating Scandinavian and Gaelic Ancestry in the Male Settlers of Iceland.* The American Society of Human Genetics Vol. 67, pp.697-717.

[99.] Helgason, Agnar,, Sigurðardóttir, Sigrún, Gulcher R. Jeffrey, Ward, Ryk and Stefansson, Kári. 2000b *mtDNA and the Origin of the Icelanders: Deciphering Signals of Recent Population History.* Am. J. Hum. Genet. 66:999–1016.

[100.] Balanovsky & Rootsi et al. 2008

[101.] Harding and Jobling 2008 p23.

## THE FALSE ANALYSIS - THE BROMBOROUGH ARGUMENT

Therefore, this author cannot give credence to the arguments[102] that, Bromborough on the Wirral was the site of *Brúnanburh,* and that *dyngesmere* was *Þingsmere*, especially when compared the evidence of the Fylde argument. As all extant sources give a hard '*d*' not a '*Þ*' to assert this claim etymologically otherwise seems' to be stretching credulity. (See page 7 of this article). Noticeably, there were *Þings* either side of the Mersey, so both from an etymological and a topographical viewpoint, as well as from the climatic maritime data this argument is untenable. Thus, we must regard the '*Þ* argument' as a fallacy.

*Brúne*[103] *(DB)* of *Burn Naze* is the correct use of the prefix *Brúnan* of *Brúnanburh* rather than *Brom, Broom* of Bromborough which is 12th century. There is another important factor in the Fylde argument which must not be overlooked – *Burn Naze was in Northumbria. Whereas Bromborough was in Mercia.* According to all sources the battle was fought in Northumbria, this is a fundamental point that cannot be overlooked. On this point alone the Bromborough argument is indefensible.

(a) The poem clearly states *Æthelstan* divided the Pagan army, *Constantine* fled North independently of *Anlaf* (*Óláf*) who fled to his longships. No such path of escape is offered by the Bromborough argument for the Scottish and Welsh forces. How could *Constantine*, King of Scots, travel overland back to Scotland from Bromborough? He would have to fight his way through *Æthelstan's* lines, then past the forts of Farndon, Chester, Eddisbury, Runcorn, Thelwell go across the Mersey, and past the fort of Manchester before he could travel North (Figure 22, p.32). Therefore, the Bromborough argument becomes totally untenable on the above major discrepancies. In conclusion, the Fylde argument is supported by manuscript, topographical and landscape evidence which are consistent in detail and emphasize the chronological and historical veracity.

(b) The projected scientific analysis of the tidal dispositions: surge, turbulence and weather conditions at the equinox by the HM Nautical Almanac Office, employing the NASA database, does support the view of the surrogate word, *dyngesmere* – 'the noisy sea' from a fluid dynamics viewpoint. When compared to historical annals a robust confirmation is endorsed of climate conditions at the time.

(c) Cartographic analysis highlights Burn Naze (DB *Brúne*) and the original name for the Fleetwood peninsula –*Berge (rode),* - hence *Brúne Berge / Brúnanburh.* Further etymological evidence of specific words -*feld* (plain), now Fylde and -*stede* (estate) corroborate this analysis identifying the coastal landscape. Also, the age and the meaning of field-names clearly demonstrate the veracity of the *Brúne Næs* site.

---

[102] Kevin Halloran rather discourteously states, "The Bromborough people have surmounted this problem (i.e. to establish a wholly convincing case) by simply dominating the media (and, regrettably the BBC) with frankly half-baked ideas. Livingstone et al resort 'imo' to the old tactic of 'it is widely accepted...etc' as a substitute for evidence." (https://senchus.wordpress.com/ Senchus 31 August 2012 – https://senchus.wordpress.com/2012/08/29/more-brunanburh-links/).

[103] The *Annales Cambriae* 1860 Ed. Rev. John Williams Ab Ithel, p17, describe the battle as "*Bellum Brune*" confirming the original name. This edition is from the 'A' MS in the British Library, Harleian 3859, folios 190r – 193r specifically fo.190ᵃ col. 2. This is the primary text, "the most ancient copy (xxviii) therefore the most historically valuable of the three copies and was written in the second half of the tenth century".

Consequently, with the three above points: **a, b, and c** and the NASA data, there are an **additional sixteen major points against** the site of Bromborough:-

(1) The literary d / Þ argument.

(2) Bromborough was in Mercia, yet all sources state the battle was fought in Northumbria – Burn (*Brúne*) Naze, the *Berry* (burgh) on the west side of the river Wyre, was in Northumbria.

(3) The Domesday Book does not mention Bromborough and its earliest reference is during the 12$^{th}$ century.

(4) Morecambe Bay has a muddy seabed, hence **ón fealene flod** - on the dusky flood tide; the seabed in the Mersey next to Bromborough is bedrock, till and sand and does not match the description in the poem. (see R.L.Folk 1954 J. Geol. 62. pp.344-359).

(5) If Bromborough was the site of a battle it is over the other side of the Wirral to the river Dee (see p.7) which has marshes at this point and the battle would have been called Heswall which overlooks those marshes. The point is that the name *Brúnanburh* should stand on its own merit. One should not have to 'fit' it into a complicated and obtuse answer.

(6) The original name for the Fleetwood peninsula before 1800 was *Bergerod*, early maps confirm this aspect: Notice the ASax: *Berg* – fort, *rod* – clearing, indicative of that age.

(7) Burn Naze (DB *Brúne*) an early seaport to the south-east of Burn Hall was on raised ground, could be fortified, and was surrounded by creeks (Annales Cambriae: "Bellum Brune").

(8) Thorpe's analysis of 'on the fallow flood' underscores a meandering river when it breaks its banks and floods the adjacent 'fringe' - the area of a 'plain'. Fluvial terraces represent ancient flooded areas formed by layers of silt and sediment, i.e. clay, silt, loam, sand, gravel. These terraces form raised islands (OIc: *Hólmr* - Holme) in the flood plain - Burn Naze is such an area.

(9) OE: –*gēfylde*: *gē* 'district'; OE: –*feld*; ModEng: *fylde* 'plain'- the district of the plain. (see p.7) *ón waelfelda* – plain of the slain. N.B. there is no 'Plain' on the Wirral.

(10) *Ón folcstede* "on the country dwelling of the folk" or "rural estate". The **stede** of Treales Old Welsh *Tref-llys* - the palace of the country folk - hence **folcstede** -the estate of the folk. Also, the (Roman) Chester field-names indicate a place of importance, the 'Holy Place' (see page 24). Just south of Treales is (Anglo-Saxon) Kirkham and running between the two is a road called Watling Street OE: **wealhas** – foreigner. This is not 'The Watling Street' but a pathway/causeway leading to Danes Pad.

(11) The Church at Lund (*lunde* – a grove) although fairly modern has within it a Roman altar on which there are images of the three mothers (*Matres*), which is a mile away from (Old Welsh) Treales.

(12) The two peculiar named Fylde causeways – Danes Pad and Kates Pad (O.Brith. *Catt - Battle path*) highlight the two escape routes from the initial battle.

(13) No path of escape is offered for the Scottish and Welsh forces at Bromborough.

(14) In order for the Scots and Welsh to join forces with the Hiberno-Norse they would have to go through Æthelstan's six forts after crossing the Mersey and *vice versa* return to the north.

(15) Amounderness/Fylde was the direct route to the kingdom of York from Dublin.

(16) Politically Amounderness/Fylde was in Æthelstan's control since AD 934 cutting off *Anlaf/ Óláfr*'s access to York but also impinged on the kingdom of Strathclyde and Rheged.

In an Age of political complexity and scarcity of primary information, the locale disappeared a few years after the battle was fought. All that remained were the allusions in the panegyric. W.D. Ross (1936: 63) cites Aristotle, "It is only the awareness of change that makes us aware of the lapse of time. Time then must be either 'change' or some element in change, and since it is not the former it must be the latter. The question is, what element?" Consequently, these allusions in the poem were constrained within the cultural moiré of time.

Above all the significance of the statement at the beginning of this article should be clearly recognized, that *'manuscript evidence is material culture'*. The changing nature of culture is the element that Aristotle questions. Written two years after the event, the poem, when scrutinized contains a descriptive analysis of maritime and landscape geography, the veracity of which is detailed in the Flyde argument. This is of paramount importance distinguishing the correct locale rather than the various place-names that sound like *Brúnanburh*. Therefore, the current argument for Bromborough cannot be sustained as to use Alistair Campbell's wise quote in 1938:

> "Unless new evidence can be produced, an honest *nescio* is greatly to be preferred to ambitious localisations built upon sand."

Subsequently, this scientific / historic evidence, verifying through coastal and landscape topographic analysis robustly corroborates the material evidence in the manuscript. This approach should be at the forefront of any research to solve the elusiveness of such a subject. Clear, robust, scrutinized evidence can now place the *Brúnanburh* locale finally and firmly on the Amounderness / Fylde peninsula.

John R. Kirby
Oxford.    28th July 2017

# BIBLIOGRAPHY

**Angus, W.S.** 1937 *The Battlefield of Brunanburh* Antiquary xi pp283-93.

**Ailred of Rievaulx,** *(Ed.)* Roger Twysden, Historiae Anglicanie Scriptores X (1652).

**Annales Cambriae** 1860 [ACam] Ed. Rev. John Williams Ab Ithel, London. Longman, Green, Longman and Roberts.

**Annals of Clonmacnoise** *from the earliest period to AD 1408* (trans. AD1627 by C. Mageoghagan, [AClon] ed. by Rev. Denis Murphy for the Royal society of Antiquaries of Ireland. Dublin, University Press. 1896, 154, 150 & 154.

**Annals of the Kingdom of Ireland by the Four Masters**, 7 vols (Dublin 1848-55) [AFM] J.P. O'Donovan (Ed & Trans), i 632 (935.16).

**Annals of Innsfallen** (Unknown author) [AI] Ed. Seán Mac Airt. *Corpus of Electronic Texts Edition.* Funded by University College, Cork and Professor Marianne McDonald via the CELT Project.

**Annals Regni Francorum** G.H. Pertzii and Fridericus Kurze [ARF] 1895 *Annals Regni Francorum. inde AB A741 usque AD A. 829 qui dicuntur Annals Laurissenses Maiores et Einhardi.* Hannoverae.

**Annals of Ulster** (to AD1131) part I Dublin 1983 [AU] 937.6, Sean Mac Airt & Gearoid Mac Niocaill (eds).

**Balanovsky, Oleg. Rootsi Siiri. Pshenichnov, Andrey., Kivisild Toomas, Churnosov Michail, Evseeva Irina, Pocheshkhova Elvira, Margarita Boldyreva Margarita, Yankovsky Nikolay, Balanovska Elena and Villems Richard** 2008 *Two Sources of the Russian Patrilineal Heritage in Their Eurasian Context* Am J Hum Genet. Jan 10; 82(1): 236–250.

**Bosworth & Toller** revised Toller 1898, *Anglo Saxon Dictionary*. O.U.P. Main Volume, p.221.

**Breeze, Andrew.** 1999 *The Battle of Brunanburh and Welsh Tradition.* Neophilologus 83: 479-482.

**British Library** MS Cotton Otho B. xi, London.

**British Library** MS Harleian 3859 folios 190r – 193r. London.

**Brockie, William.** 1886 *Legends and Superstitions in the County of Durham.*114.

**Brooks, William M.** 1885 *The Antiquary: a magazine devoted to the study of the past.* (Oct) Vol XII London: Elliot Stock.

**Camden, William.** 1607 Britannia (trans.) Philemon Holland Hypetext (ed.), Sutton, D.F. (2004).

**Cameron, Kenneth** 1961 *English Place-Names.* B.T. Batsford Ltd. London.

**Campbell, Alistair** 1938 *The Battle of Brunanburh,* London.

**Cavill, Paul, Harding, Stephen & Jesch, Judith** 2004 *Revisiting Dingesmere.* Journal of the English Place-Name Society xxxvi pp25-38.

**Cavill, Paul** 2008 *The site of the Battle of Brunanburh: manuscripts and maps, grammar and geography.* In A Commodity of Good Names: Essays in honour of Margaret Gelling (eds.) Padel, O.J. & Parsons, D.N., Shaun Tyas, Donington.

**Christison, David** 1899 *Account of the Excavation of the camps and earthworks at Birrenswark Hill, in Annan Dale, undertaken by the society in 1898.* Proceedings of the Society of Antiquaries of Scotland. pp198-218.

**Chronicle of Henry of Huntingdon,** Trans. & Ed. Thomas Forester, (1853) London.

**Cleasby, R., Vígfússon, G. and Craigie, R.** 1957 (2nd Ed.) *Icelandic English Dictionary.* O.U.P.

**Cockburn, John H.** 1931 *The battle of Brunanburgh and its period elucidated by place-names.* London & Sheffield.

Collins RN, Captain Greenville 1689 *Great Britain's Coastal Pilot: Fylde Coast.*

Crawford, Osbert Guy Stanhope 1934 *The Battle of Brunanburh.* Antiquity V.A.Bol. 8 No.31 (Sept) pp338-9.

Deacon, Margaret 1971 *Scientists and the Sea 1650-1900.* London: Academic Press.

Dera, Jerzy 1992 *Marine Physics.* Elsevier Oceanography Series 53 Oxford. Polish Scientific Pub. Warszowa. *Chapt. 8 The Acoustic Properties of the Sea.*

**Ding L., Farmer D.,** 1993 *Passive acoustical measurements of scale, probability, and intensity of wave breaking,* OCEANS '93 – Engineering in harmony with ocean, IEEE Proc., Vol. 2, II-193-197.

**Dodgson, John McN.** 1957 *The Background of Brunanburh.* Saga Book of the Viking Society for Northern Research. 14:4 pp303-16.

**Dodgson, John McN.** 1972 Place-Names of Cheshire 4, 240.

**Dodgson, John McN.** 1997 Addenda and Corrigenda Place-Names of Cheshire 5-2, xxi.

# BIBLIOGRAPHY - continued

**Eisner, Ma**rtin. 2014 *In the Labyrinth of the Library: Petrarch's Cicero, Dante's Virgil and the Historiography of the Renaissance.* Renaissance Quarterly 67 755-90.

**Ekwall, Eilert** 1922 *Place Names of Lancashire.* Manchester University Press.

**Environment Agency** 2011 *Coastal Flood Boundary Conditions for UK mainland and islands Project: SC060064/TR2:* Design sea-levels Flood and Coastal Erosion Risk Management Research and Development Programme, Authors: A. McMillian, C. Batstone, D. Worth, J. Tawn, K. Horsburgh, M. Lawless.

**Farrer, William** (ed.) 1914 *Early Yorkshire Charters.*Vol.1, Edinburgh.

**Faux. David K.** 2008 A Genetic Signal of Central European Celtic Ancestry: Preliminary Research Concerning Y-Chromosomal Marker U152 (Part 2) Hallstatt Culture: 720 to 600 BC and 600 BC to 480 BC (Ha C and D). http://www.davidkfaux.org/files/LaTene_Celt_R1b1c10_part2.pdf

**Fellows-Jensen, Gillian** 1991 *Scandinavians in Dumfriesshire and Galloway: the place-name evidence.* pp. 77-96, in *Celtic Norse Relationships in the Irish Sea in the Middle Ages 800-1200.* Eds Jón Viðar Sigurðsson and Timothy Bolton Brill, Leiden 2014.

**Folk, R.L.** 1954 *The Distinction between Grain Size and Mineral Composition in Sedimentary-Rock Nomenclature* J. Geol. 62, No.4 (July) pp344-359.

**Foot, Sarah** 2011 *Æthelstan - the first king of England.* Yale University Press. New Haven & London.

**Fox, Samuel Rev.** 1864 *King Alfred's Anglo-Saxon Version of Boethius de Consolatione Philosophiae with a literal English translation, notes and glossary.* Bohn Antiquarian Library, London.

**Gale, Roger.** 1737 *Stukeley's Letters and Diaries.* Surtees Society (ed.) W.C.Lukis Durham, III, p.140, mentioned by Sir John Clerk in his letters to Rev. William Stukeley.

**Garmonsway, George N. (trans.)** 1965 *The Anglo-Saxon Chronicle.* J. M. Dent & Sons;

**Garmonsway, George N. (trans.)** 1975 *The Anglo-Saxon Chronicle - The Laud (Peterborough) Chronicle.* Bodleian MS. Laud 636.

**Garnett, James M.** 1889, ed. 1900 *Elene; Judith; Athelstan, or the fight at Brunanburh; Byrhtnoth, or the fight at Maldon; and the Dream of the Rood: Anglo-Saxon Poems.* Boston

**Goodall, Armitage** 1914 *Place-Names in southwest Yorkshire.* Cambridge University Press, 312-313.

**Guest, Edwin.** 1838 *History of English Rhythms.* Vol II London, William Pickering.

**Halloran, Kevin,** 2005 *The Brunanburh Campaign: A Reappraisal,* Scottish Historical Review Vol. LXXXIV, 2: No. 218 (October), 146.

**Hamson R.M.** 1985 *"The theoretical response of vertical and horizontal line arrays to wind induced noise in shallow water"* [J. Acoust. Soc. Am. Vol.78 (5), pp1702–1709].

**Harding, S., Jobling, M.** 2008 *Vikings.* British Archaeology. (Nov-Dec).

**Harrison, Kenneth** 1983 *A note on the Battle of Brunanburh (in Browney Valley),* Durham Archaeology I pp63-65.

**Hart, Cyril.** 1992 *The Danelaw.* The Hambledon Press, London & Rio Grande.

**Hart, Cyril R**. 1975 *The Early Charters of Northern England and the North Midlands.* Leicester. Chapter VII. No.119. p117.

**Haugen, Einar** 1976 *The Scandinavian Languages: an introduction to their history.* Faber & Faber. London.6.3. (10). p73.

**Heale Grandon** 2006 *'Fylde and Wyre Antiquarian Society'* (March).

**Helgason, Agnar,, Sigurðardóttir, Sigrún,**

**Gulcher R. Jeffrey, Ward Ryk and Stefansson, Kári.** 2000 *mtDNA and the Origin of the Icelanders: Deciphering Signals of Recent Population History* Am. J. Hum. Genet. 66:999–1016, 2000.

**Helgason, Agnar, Sigurðardóttir, S., Nicholson, J., Sykes, B., Hill, E., Bradley, D., Bosnes, V., Gulcher, J., Ward, R., and Stefánsson, K.** 2000 *Estimating Scandinavian and Gaelic Ancestry in the Male Settlers of Iceland.* The American Society of Human Genetics Vol. 67, pp697-717.

# BIBLIOGRAPHY - continued

**Helgason Agnar, Hickey Eileen, Goodacre Sara, Bosnes Vidar, Stefánsson Kári, Ward Ryk and Sykes Bryan.** 2001 *mtDNA and the Islands of the North Atlantic: Estimating the Proportions of Norse and Gaelic Ancestry* Am. J. Hum. Genet. 68:723–737.

**Higham, Nicholas J.** 1997 *The Context of Brunanburh. Names, Places and People: an Onomastic Miscellany in Memory of John McNeal Dodgson.* Ed. A.R. Rumble and A.D. Mills. Stamford.

**Hodgkin, Thomas** 1885 *Burnswark.* Athenaeum. Aug. No. 22. p239.

**HM Nautical Almanac Office,** 2011-12 *Data - Morecambe Bay for the year AD937.* Admiralty Way, Taunton, specifically Christopher Jones (Head of Tides), Steve Cooper and George Huish for work done on predicted tidal disposition and resonance. (Lic. Ref. No.557909 Jan 2012).

**Joyce, P.W.** 1910 -13 *The Origin and History of Irish Names of Places,* 3 vols, Dublin.

**Isakovich, M.A. &.Kur'yanov, B.F.** 1970 "*Theory of Low Frequency Noise in the Ocean,*" Soy. Phys. Acoust. **16**, 49-58.

**Kennedy R.M.,** 1992, *Sea surface sound dipole source dependence on wave-breaking variables,* J. Acoust. Soc. Am., 91 (4), 1974–1982.

**Kirby, John R.** 2013 *Early Settlements and their related vills on the Furness peninsula - Dalton parish c. AD800-1200.* Unpublished Post Graduate Dissertation in Archaeology, University of Oxford.

**Klusekl, Zygmunt and Lisimenka, Aliaksandr** 2013 *Acoustic noise generation under plunging breaking waves\** OCEANOLOGIA, 55 (4), pp809–836. Institute of Oceanology, Polish Academy of Sciences,Powstańcow Warszawy 55, 81-712 Sopot, Poland & Maritime Institute in Gdańsk, Długi Targ 41/42, 80-830 Gdańsk, Poland;

**Klusek Z., Jakacki J.,** 1997 *On the concentrations of gas bubbles measured acoustically in the Baltic Sea - wind and time dependences,* Proc. Int. Symp. Hydroacoust. Ultrasonics, EAA Symposium (formerly 13th FASE Symposium), Jurata, May 1997, A. Stepnowski & E. Kozaczka (eds.), pp103–108.

**Kolaini A.R.,** 1998, *Sound radiation by various types of laboratory breaking waves in fresh and salt water,* J. Acoust. Soc. Am., 103 (1), pp300–308.

**.Landnámabók.** Guðbrand Vigfússon and F. York Powell. 1905 *Origines Islandicae.* Vol 1, Oxford.

**Lennon, Geoffrey W.** 1963 *The identification of weather conditions associated with the generation of major storm surges along the west coast of the British Isles.* Q.J.R. Meteorol. Soc., 89, pp381-394.

**Liddle, Henry G. & Scott, Robert** 1883 *Greek-English Lexicon.* New York: 858ab

**Livingstone. Michael,** 2011 *The Battle of Brunanburh: a casebook.* University of Exeter Press. pp. xi-xii.

**Loewen M.R., Melville W.K.,** 1994, *An experimental investigation of the collective oscillations of bubble plumes entrained by breaking waves,* J. Acoust. Soc. Am., 95, pp1329–1343.

**Magoun, Francis Peabody** 1933 *Cockburn: the battle of Brunanburh and its period elucidated by place-names.* 86 n.1.

**Makris N. C., Wilson J.D.,** 2008, *Quantifying hurricane destructive power, wind speed, and air-sea material exchange with natural undersea sound,* Geophys. Res. Let., 35 (10), L10603.

**Mason, D. C., Amin, M., Davenport, I. J., Flather, R. A., Robinson, G. J., Smith, J. A.,** 1999. *Measurement of Recent Intertidal Sediment Transport in Morecambe Bay using the Waterline Method.* Estuarine, Coastal and Shelf Science 49, pp427–456.

**Mitsuyasu, H. & Honda, T.** 1974 " *The High-Frequency Spectrum of Wind-Generated Waves,*" J. Oceanogr. Soc. Jpn. **30**, pp29-42.

**Mommsen, Theodore E.** "Petrarch's Conception of the 'Dark Ages'" *Speculum* **17**.2 (April 1942: 226–242).

**Morton, Jamie.** 2001 *The Role of the Physical Environment in Ancient Greek Seafaring.* Brill, Leiden, :31.

**Neilson, George** 1909 *Brunanburh & Burnswark.* Scottish Historical Review VII, pp37-55.

**Oguz H.N.** 1994 "*A theoretical study of low-frequency oceanic ambient noise.*" [J. Acoust. Soc. Am., Vol. 95 (4), pp. 1895–1912].

**Orkneyinga Saga,** Paul Edwards tr. with Hermann Pálsson 1978 *Orkneyinga saga: the history of the Earls of Orkney,* London: Hogarth Press,

# BIBLIOGRAPHY - continued

**Orris G. J., Nicholas M.,** 2000, *Collective oscillations of fresh and salt water bubble plumes*, J. Acoust. Soc. Am., 107 (2), pp771–787.

**Porter, John** 1876 *History of the Fylde of Lancashire.* Fleetwood & Blackpool: W. Porter & Sons Pub

**Pugh, David T. & Thompson K.R.** 1986 *The Subtidal behaviour of the Celtic Sea – 1 Sea level and bottom pressures.* Continental Shelf Research 5 pp293-319.

**Pugh. David T.** 1987 (rept. 1996) *Tides, Surges and Mean Sea-level.* Natural Environment Research Council, Swindon UK.

**Rivet, A.L.F. & Smith, Colin** 1979 *The Place-Names of Roman Britain.* Batsford Ltd, London.

**Roger of Wendover,** *Flowers of History. The History of England from the descent of the Saxons to AD1235 formerly ascribed to Matthew Paris.* Trans. By J.A. Giles Vol 1 (1849) London.

**Ross, W.D.** 1936 $API\Sigma TOTE\Lambda Y\Sigma\ \Phi Y\Sigma IKH\ AKPOA\Sigma I\Sigma$ -- *Aristotle's Physics* Oxford, Clarendon Press.

**Rosser, Zoë. H. Zerjal, Tatiana. Hurles, Matthew E. Adojaan, Maarja. Alavantic, Dragan. Amorim, António. Amos, William. Armenteros, Manuel. Arroyo, Eduardo. Barbujani, Guido. Beckman, Gunhild. Lars Beckman, Lars. Bertranpetit, Jaume. Bosch, Elena. Bradley, Daniel G. Brede, Gaute. Cooper, Gillian. Côrte-Real, Helena B.S.M. Knijff, Peter de. Decorte, Ronny. Dubrova, Yuri E. Evgrafov, Oleg. Gilissen, Anja. Glisic, Sanja. Gölge, Mukaddes. Hill, Emmeline W. Jeziorowska, Anna. Kalaydjieva, Luba. Kayser, Manfred. Kivisild, Toomas. Kravchenko, Sergey A. Krumina, Astrida. Kučinskas, Vaidutis. Lavinha, João. Livshits, Ludmila A. Malaspina, Patrizia. Maria, Syrrou. McElreavey, Ken. Meitinger, Thomas A. Mikelsaar, Aavo-Valdur. Mitchell, R. John. Nafa, Khedoudja. Nicholson, Jayne. Nørby, Søren. Pandya, Arpita. Parik, Jüri. Patsalis, Philippos C. Pereira, Luísa. Peterlin, Borut. Pielberg, Gerli. Prata, Maria João. Previderé, Carlo. Roewer, Lutz. Rootsi, Siiri. Rubinsztein, D.C. Saillard, Juliette. Santos, Fabrício R. Stefanescu, Gheorghe. Sykes, Bryan C. Tolun, Aslihan. Villems, Richard. Tyler-Smith, Chris. Jobling Mark A.** 2000 *Y-Chromosomal Diversity in Europe Is Clinal and Influenced Primarily by Geography, Rather than by Language* "The American Journal of Human Genetics" Volume 67, Issue 6, December, pp1526–1543.

**Sawyer, P. H.** 1968 *Anglo-Saxon Charters. An Annotated List and Bibliography*, Royal Historical Society Guides & Handbooks, 8 London No.520.

***Scottish National Dictionary*** (eds) William Grant (1929-1946) and David Murison (1946-1976).

**Semino, Ornella. Passarino, Giuseppe. Oefner, Peter J. Lin, Alice A. Arbuzova, Svetlana. Beckman, Lars E. De Benedictis, Giovanna. Francalacci, Paolo. Kouvatsi, Anastasia. Limborska, Svetlana. Marcikiæ, Mladen. Mika, Anna. Mika, Barbara. Primorac, Dragan. Santachiara-Benerecetti, A. Silvana. Cavalli-Sforza, L. Luca.**

**Underhill, Peter A.** 2000 *The Genetic Legacy of Paleolithic* Homo sapiens sapiens *in Extant Europeans: A Y Chromosome Perspective.* Science 10 Nov 2000:Vol. 290, Issue 5494, pp1155-1159.

**Smith, Albert H.** 1937 *The Site of the Battle of Brunanburh.* ed. R.W.Chambers, F. Norman, & A.H.Smith. London Medieval Studies. I, pp56-9.

**Smyth, Alfred P.** 1979 *Scandinavian York & Dublin, the History and Archaeology of Two Related Viking Kingdoms.* Vol. 2, Humanities Press: New Jersey & Templekieran Press: Dublin.

**Sykes, B.C.** 2006 Blood of the Isles. Bantam Press, A division of Transworld Publishing, Random House Group, London.

**Thorpe, Benjamin** 1834 *Analecta Anglo-Saxonica.* London.

**Thorpe, Benjamin** 1848 (ed.) [FofW] *Florentii Wigorniensis Monachi Chronicon ex Chronicis.* English Historical Society, I, 132.

**Thorpe, Benjamin** 1861 *Anglo-Saxon Chronicles Ed Benjamin Thorpe Vol II,* London, pp86-88.

**Toller, T. Northcote** 1921, *Anglo Saxon Dictionary Supplement.* O.U.P. p162.

**Wainwright, Frederick T.** 1975 *Scandinavian England.* Ed. H.P.R. Finberg. Philimore.

# BIBLIOGRAPHY - continued

**West, Thomas.** [died 1779] *The Antiquities of Furness or an Account of the Royal Abbey of St. Mary, in the Vale of Nightshade, near Dalton in Furness.* Pub. by Rt. Hon. Lord George Cavendish (no date but pub. privately 1774).

**Whitaker, John** 1771 *History of Manchester in four books,* Vol. 1, p125.

**Whitelock, D.** 1940 *The Modern Language Review,* Vol. 35, No. 1 (Jan.,), pp78-80.

**Whitelock, D.** (ed.) 1955 *English Historical Documents I c. 500 – 1042.* No's. 41 & 104.

**Wilkinson, Thomas Turner** 1864 *Brunanburh (Burnley).* Notes and Queries VI page 342.

**Wilson J.F., Weiss Deborah A., Richards Martin, Thomas, Mark.G., Bradman Neil, Goldstein David B.,** 2001 *Genetic evidence for different male and female roles during Cultural transitions in the British Isles.* April. PNAS vol 98 No.9, pp5078-5083.

**Wilson, J.H.** 1979 *"Very low frequency (VLF) wind-generated noise produced by turbulent pressure fluctuations in the atmosphere near the ocean surface,"* [J. Acoust. Soc. Am. Vol. 66(5) Nov, pp1499].

**Wolf, Judith** 2009 *Coastal Flooding: Impacts of coupled wave-surge-tide models.* Nat. Hazards 49, pp241-260.

**Wood, Fergus J.** 1986 *Tidal Dynamics, Coastal Flooding and Cycles of Gravitational Force.* Dordrecht: D. Reidel.

**Wood, Michael** 1980 *Brunanburh Revisited.* Saga Book of the Viking Society xx.3 pp200-17.

**Wood, Michael** 2013 *Searching for Brunanburh: the Yorkshire Context of the 'Great War' of 937.* Yorks. Arch. Journal 85, pp138-59.

**Wright, Joseph.** 1898 *The English Dialect Dictionary: being the complete vocabulary of all dialect words still in use or known to have been in use during the last two hundred years.* Vol. 1, A-C, Henry Frowde. Oxford, London & New York.

**Yang T.C. & Kwang Yoo** 1997 *"Modeling the environment influence on the vertical directionality of ambient noise in shallow water"* [J. Acoust. Soc. Am., Vol. 101(5), pp2541–2554.

| | |
|---|---|
| 40 hár hildering. hreman ne þorfte. | hoary warrior. He had no reason to exult |
| mæcan gemanan. he wæs his mæga sceard. | the great meeting; he was of his kinsmen bereft, |
| freonda gefylled. on folcstede. | friends fell on the battle-field, |
| beslagen æt sæcce. 7 his sunu forlet. | killed at strife: even his son, young in battle, he left |
| on wælstowe. wundum fergrunden. | in the place of slaughter, ground to pieces with wounds. |
| 45 giungne æt guðe. gelpan ne þorfte. | That grizzle-haired warrior had no |
| beorn blandenfeax. bilgeslehtes, | reason to boast of sword-slaughter, |
| eald inwidda. ne anlaf þy ma. | old deceitful one, no more did Anlaf; |
| mid heora herelafu. hlehhan ne þorftun. | with their remnant of an army they had no reason to |
| þæt hie beaduweorca. beterþan wurdun. | laugh that they were better in deed of war |
| 50 ón campstede. cumlbodgehnades. | in battle-field--collision of banners, |
| garmittinge. gumena gemotes. | encounter of spears, encounter of men, |
| wæpengewrixles. þæs hi ón wælfelda. | trading of blows--when they played against |
| wiþ eadweardes. afaran plegodan. | the sons of Eadweard on the battle field. |
| gewitan him þa norþmenn. nægledcnearrū. | Departed then the Northmen in nailed ships. |
| 55 dreorig daroða laf. ón dingesmere. | dejected survivors of battle, in Dingesmere |
| ofer deop wæter. difel in secan. | over waters deep sought Dublin, |
| 7eft hira land. æwiscmode. | to return to Ireland, ashamed in spirit. |
| swilce þa gebroþor. begen ætsamne. | Likewise the brothers, both together, |
| cyning 7 æþeling. cyþþe sohton. | King and Prince, sought their home, |
| 60 wesseaxena land. wiges hraemige. | West-Saxon land, exultant from battle. |
| letan him behindan. hræw bryttian. | They left behind them, to enjoy the corpses, |
| saluwigpadan. þone sweartan hræfn. | the dark coated one, the dark horny-beaked raven |
| hyrnednebban. 7 þane hasewanpadan. | and the dusky-coated one, |
| earn æftan hwit. æses brucan. | the eagle white from behind, to partake of carrion, |
| 65 grædigne guðhafóc. 7 þæt græge deor. | greedy war-hawk, and that gray animal |
| wulf ón wealde. | the wolf in the forest. |
| ne wearð wæl mare. | Never was there more slaughter |
| ón þys eiglande. æfre gieta. | on this island, never yet as many |
| folces gefylled. beforan þissū. | people killed before this |
| 70 sweordes écgum. Þæs þe us secgað béc. | with sword's edge: never according to those who tell us |
| ealde uðwitan. siþþan eastan hider. | from books, old wisemen, |
| engle 7 seaxe. up becoman. | since from the east Angles and Saxons came up |
| ofer brad brimu. brytene sohtan, | over the broad sea. Britain they sought, |
| wlance wigsmiþas. weealas ofercoman. | Proud war-smiths who overcame the Welsh, |
| 75 eorlas arhwate. eard begeataN. | glorious warriors they took hold of the land. |